TEACHER'S PET PUBLICATIONS

PUZZLE PACK
for
Julius Caesar

based on the book by
William Shakespeare

Written by
William T. Collins

© 2005 Teacher's Pet Publications
All Rights Reserved

The materials in this packet are copyrighted by Teacher's Pet Publications, Inc.

These pages may be duplicated by the purchaser for use in the purchaser's own classroom.

Copying any of these materials and distributing them for any other purpose is a violation of the copyright laws.

© 2005 Teacher's Pet Publications, Inc.
www.tpet.com

INTRODUCTION
If you already own the LitPlan for this title, this Puzzle Pack will refresh your Unit Resource Materials and Vocabulary Resource Materials sections plus give you additional materials you can substitute into the tests. If you do not already have a complete LitPlan, these pages will give you some supplemental materials to use with your own plan. There are two main groups of materials: one set for unit words (such as characters' names, symbols, places, etc.) and one set for vocabulary words associated with the book.

WORD LIST
There is a word list for both the unit words and the vocabulary words. These lists show you which words are being used in the materials and the clues or definitions being used for those words. You may want to give students a word list with clues/definitions to help them, or you may want students to only have a word list (without clues/definitions) if you want them to work a little harder. Both are available for duplication. The word lists can also be your "calling key" for the bingo games.

FILL IN THE BLANK AND MATCHING
There are 4 each of the fill in the blank and matching worksheets for both the unit and vocabulary words. These pages can be used either as extra worksheets for students or as objective parts of a unit test. They can be done individually if students need extra help or as a whole class activity to review the material covered.

MAGIC SQUARES
The magic squares not only reinforce the material covered but also work on reasoning and math skills. Many teachers have told us that their students really enjoy doing these!

WORD SEARCH PUZZLES
The word search words go in all directions, as indicated on your answer keys. Two of the word search puzzles have the clues listed rather than the words. This makes the puzzle a little more difficult, but it reinforces the material better. Two word search puzzles have words only for students who find the clue puzzles too difficult.

CROSSWORD PUZZLES
Both unit and vocabulary word sections have 4 crossword puzzles.

BINGO CARDS
There are 32 individual bingo cards for the unit words and 32 individual bingo cards for the vocabulary words. You can use your word list as a "call list," calling the words at random and marking them off of your list as you go, or you could use the flash cards by cutting them apart and drawing the words at random from a hat (or box or whatever). To make a better review, you might ask for the definition and spelling of each word as you call it out—or you could call out the definitions and have students tell you the words they need to look for on the puzzle.

JUGGLE LETTERS
The vocabulary juggle letter game is intended to help students learn the spellings of the words. One sheet has the definitions listed on it as an extra help for students who need it or to reinforce the definitions if you choose to do so.

FLASH CARDS
We've included a set of vocabulary flash cards you can duplicate, cut, and fold for your students. Some teachers make a few sets for general use by the class; others make a set for each student. Some teachers duplicate them for each student and have the students cut & fold their own. You can cut out just the words and put them in a hat, have each student pick out one word and write the definition and a sentence for that word. Students then swap words and papers, with the next student adding a sentence of his own under the last one. You can have students swap as many times as you like. Each time the student will read the sentences written prior to his own and then add a sentence. You can cut out the words and definitions separately and play "I Have; Who Has?" Each student in the room draws a word and definition. The first student says, "I have (the name of the word). Who has the definition?" The student with the definition reads it then says, "I have (the name of the vocabulary word she has). Who has the definition?" The round continues until all words and definitions have been given.

Julius Caesar Word List

No.	Word	Clue/Definition
1.	ANTONY	Devoted follower of Caesar; defeats Brutus
2.	ARTEMIDORUS	Gives Caesar a letter of warning naming the conspirators
3.	BRUTUS	Joins and then leads the conspiracy to kill Caesar
4.	BUTCHERS	Let us be sacrificers, but not ____, Caius.
5.	CALPURNIA	Caesar's wife
6.	CASCA	First to stab Caesar
7.	CASSIUS	Organizes the conspiracy & gets Brutus to join
8.	CATO	Soldier in army of Brutus & Cassius
9.	CICERO	Roman Senator to whom Casca talks on the eve of the assassination
10.	CINNA	Plants the forged letter for Cassius
11.	CLITUS	Servant of Brutus; refused to kill Brutus
12.	CONSPIRACY	An agreement to perform together an illegal act
13.	CROWN	Antony offered Caesar one
14.	DECIUS	Reinterprets Calpurnia's dream and convinces Caesar to go to Senate
15.	DREAMS	Calpurnia tries to convince Caesar that her ____ are omens of tragedy
16.	FLAVIUS	Tribune who breaks up crowd waiting to honor Caesar's triumph
17.	FRIENDS	____, Romans, countrymen, lend me your ears.
18.	FUNERAL	Antony spoke at Caesar's
19.	HUNGRY	Yond Cassius has a lean and ____ look.
20.	JULIUS	____ Caesar
21.	LEPIDUS	Joins with Octavius and Antony and is used by them
22.	LIGARIUS	Vows to follow Brutus
23.	LUCILIUS	Captured by Antony's soldiers, mistaken for Brutus
24.	LUCIUS	Servant to Brutus
25.	MAN	... that Nature might stand up/And say to all the world, 'This was a ____'
26.	MARCH	Beware the Ides of ____
27.	MESSALA	Reports Portia's death, discovers Cassius's body
28.	METELLUS	Distracts Caesar's attention so conspirators can carry out their plan
29.	MIGHT	I have a man's mind, but a woman's ____.
30.	MIGHTY	O Julius Caesar, thou art ____ yet.
31.	MISCHIEF	____, thou art afoot, Take thou what course thou wilt.
32.	MURDER	Help, ho! They ____ Caesar!
33.	OATH	Brutus thinks a just cause needs no ____ to bind the doers to their cause
34.	OCTAVIUS	Heir of Julius Caesar
35.	PAPILIUS	Wishes Cassius well in his 'enterprise'
36.	PINDARUS	Servant to Cassius
37.	PORTIA	Wife of Brutus
38.	PUBLIUS	One of many who escort Caesar to the Senate meeting
39.	ROME	... not that I loved Caesar less, but that I loved ____ more
40.	SENATE	Caesar goes to this meeting
41.	SOOTHSAYER	Warns Caesar to 'Beware the Ides of March'
42.	STRATO	Holds Brutus's suicide sword
43.	SWORD	Caesar, thou art revenged, Even with the ____ that killed thee.
44.	TITINIUS	Officer, guards tent at Sardis
45.	TREBONIUS	Takes Antony away from the assassination scene so he won't interfere

Copyrighted

Julius Caesar Word List

No.	Word	Clue/Definition
46.	TYRANNY	Liberty! Freedom! ____ is dead!
47.	VARRO	Servant of Brutus
48.	VOLUMNIUS	Friend & soldier to Brutus; refuses to hold Brutus's sword
49.	WIFE	Render me worthy of this noble ____!
50.	WILL	Caesar, now be still. I killed not thee with half so good a ____.

Julius Caesar Fill In The Blanks 1

_____

1. Takes Antony away from the assassination scene so he won't interfere
2. Yond Cassius has a lean and ___ look.
3. Caesar goes to this meeting
4. ... that Nature might stand up/And say to all the world, 'This was a ___'
5. Joins with Octavius and Antony and is used by them
6. Help, ho! They ____ Caesar!
7. Distracts Caesar's attention so conspirators can carry out their plan
8. First to stab Caesar
9. Captured by Antony's soldiers, mistaken for Brutus
10. Antony spoke at Caesar's
11. An agreement to perform together an illegal act
12. Servant to Brutus
13. Render me worthy of this noble ____!
14. Liberty! Freedom! ____ is dead!
15. ____, thou art afoot, Take thou what course thou wilt.
16. ... not that I loved Caesar less, but that I loved ___ more
17. Antony offered Caesar one
18. Caesar, now be still. I killed not thee with half so good a ____.
19. Wife of Brutus
20. O Julius Caesar, thou art ____ yet.

Julius Caesar Fill In The Blanks 1 Answer Key

TREBONIUS	1. Takes Antony away from the assassination scene so he won't interfere
HUNGRY	2. Yond Cassius has a lean and ___ look.
SENATE	3. Caesar goes to this meeting
MAN	4. ... that Nature might stand up/And say to all the world, 'This was a ___'
LEPIDUS	5. Joins with Octavius and Antony and is used by them
MURDER	6. Help, ho! They ____ Caesar!
METELLUS	7. Distracts Caesar's attention so conspirators can carry out their plan
CASCA	8. First to stab Caesar
LUCILIUS	9. Captured by Antony's soldiers, mistaken for Brutus
FUNERAL	10. Antony spoke at Caesar's
CONSPIRACY	11. An agreement to perform together an illegal act
LUCIUS	12. Servant to Brutus
WIFE	13. Render me worthy of this noble ____!
TYRANNY	14. Liberty! Freedom! ____ is dead!
MISCHIEF	15. ____, thou art afoot, Take thou what course thou wilt.
ROME	16. ... not that I loved Caesar less, but that I loved ___ more
CROWN	17. Antony offered Caesar one
WILL	18. Caesar, now be still. I killed not thee with half so good a ____.
PORTIA	19. Wife of Brutus
MIGHTY	20. O Julius Caesar, thou art ____ yet.

Julius Caesar Fill In The Blanks 2

_____   1. Beware the Ides of ___

_____   2. Warns Caesar to 'Beware the Ides of March'

_____   3. Plants the forged letter for Cassius

_____   4. Render me worthy of this noble ____!

_____   5. Gives Caesar a letter of warning naming the conspirators

_____   6. An agreement to perform together an illegal act

_____   7. Servant of Brutus

_____   8. Reports Portia's death, discovers Cassius's body

_____   9. ____, thou art afoot, Take thou what course thou wilt.

_____   10. Caesar's wife

_____   11. Devoted follower of Caesar; defeats Brutus

_____   12. Reinterprets Calpurnia's dream and convinces Caesar to go to Senate

_____   13. Calpurnia tries to convince Caesar that her ____ are omens of tragedy

_____   14. I have a man's mind, but a woman's ____.

_____   15. Friend & soldier to Brutus; refuses to hold Brutus's sword

_____   16. Servant of Brutus; refused to kill Brutus

_____   17. Joins with Octavius and Antony and is used by them

_____   18. Officer, guards tent at Sardis

_____   19. First to stab Caesar

_____   20. ... not that I loved Caesar less, but that I loved ___ more

Julius Caesar Fill In The Blanks 2 Answer Key

MARCH	1. Beware the Ides of ___
SOOTHSAYER	2. Warns Caesar to 'Beware the Ides of March'
CINNA	3. Plants the forged letter for Cassius
WIFE	4. Render me worthy of this noble ___!
ARTEMIDORUS	5. Gives Caesar a letter of warning naming the conspirators
CONSPIRACY	6. An agreement to perform together an illegal act
VARRO	7. Servant of Brutus
MESSALA	8. Reports Portia's death, discovers Cassius's body
MISCHIEF	9. ___, thou art afoot, Take thou what course thou wilt.
CALPURNIA	10. Caesar's wife
ANTONY	11. Devoted follower of Caesar; defeats Brutus
DECIUS	12. Reinterprets Calpurnia's dream and convinces Caesar to go to Senate
DREAMS	13. Calpurnia tries to convince Caesar that her ___ are omens of tragedy
MIGHT	14. I have a man's mind, but a woman's ___.
VOLUMNIUS	15. Friend & soldier to Brutus; refuses to hold Brutus's sword
CLITUS	16. Servant of Brutus; refused to kill Brutus
LEPIDUS	17. Joins with Octavius and Antony and is used by them
TITINIUS	18. Officer, guards tent at Sardis
CASCA	19. First to stab Caesar
ROME	20. ... not that I loved Caesar less, but that I loved ___ more

Julius Caesar Fill In The Blanks 3

_____

_____

_____

_____

_____

_____

_____

_____

_____

_____

_____

_____

_____

_____

_____

_____

_____

_____

_____

_____

1. Help, ho! They ____ Caesar!

2. Organizes the conspiracy & gets Brutus to join

3. Caesar, now be still. I killed not thee with half so good a ____.

4. Distracts Caesar's attention so conspirators can carry out their plan

5. Caesar goes to this meeting

6. Vows to follow Brutus

7. Warns Caesar to 'Beware the Ides of March'

8. Gives Caesar a letter of warning naming the conspirators

9. Devoted follower of Caesar; defeats Brutus

10. An agreement to perform together an illegal act

11. ... that Nature might stand up/And say to all the world, 'This was a ___'

12. Servant to Brutus

13. Servant of Brutus; refused to kill Brutus

14. Joins with Octavius and Antony and is used by them

15. O Julius Caesar, thou art ____ yet.

16. ... not that I loved Caesar less, but that I loved ___ more

17. ____, thou art afoot, Take thou what course thou wilt.

18. Brutus thinks a just cause needs no ___ to bind the doers to their cause

19. Tribune who breaks up crowd waiting to honor Caesar's triumph

20. Antony spoke at Caesar's

Julius Caesar Fill In The Blanks 3 Answer Key

MURDER	1. Help, ho! They _____ Caesar!
CASSIUS	2. Organizes the conspiracy & gets Brutus to join
WILL	3. Caesar, now be still. I killed not thee with half so good a _____.
METELLUS	4. Distracts Caesar's attention so conspirators can carry out their plan
SENATE	5. Caesar goes to this meeting
LIGARIUS	6. Vows to follow Brutus
SOOTHSAYER	7. Warns Caesar to 'Beware the Ides of March'
ARTEMIDORUS	8. Gives Caesar a letter of warning naming the conspirators
ANTONY	9. Devoted follower of Caesar; defeats Brutus
CONSPIRACY	10. An agreement to perform together an illegal act
MAN	11. ... that Nature might stand up/And say to all the world, 'This was a ___'
LUCIUS	12. Servant to Brutus
CLITUS	13. Servant of Brutus; refused to kill Brutus
LEPIDUS	14. Joins with Octavius and Antony and is used by them
MIGHTY	15. O Julius Caesar, thou art _____ yet.
ROME	16. ... not that I loved Caesar less, but that I loved ___ more
MISCHIEF	17. _____, thou art afoot, Take thou what course thou wilt.
OATH	18. Brutus thinks a just cause needs no ___ to bind the doers to their cause
FLAVIUS	19. Tribune who breaks up crowd waiting to honor Caesar's triumph
FUNERAL	20. Antony spoke at Caesar's

Julius Caesar Fill In The Blanks 4

_____ 1. Vows to follow Brutus

_____ 2. Joins with Octavius and Antony and is used by them

_____ 3. First to stab Caesar

_____ 4. Plants the forged letter for Cassius

_____ 5. Reinterprets Calpurnia's dream and convinces Caesar to go to Senate

_____ 6. Officer, guards tent at Sardis

_____ 7. Reports Portia's death, discovers Cassius's body

_____ 8. Joins and then leads the conspiracy to kill Caesar

_____ 9. Gives Caesar a letter of warning naming the conspirators

_____ 10. ____, thou art afoot, Take thou what course thou wilt.

_____ 11. Captured by Antony's soldiers, mistaken for Brutus

_____ 12. An agreement to perform together an illegal act

_____ 13. Servant to Cassius

_____ 14. Let us be sacrificers, but not ____, Caius.

_____ 15. Yond Cassius has a lean and ___ look.

_____ 16. Wife of Brutus

_____ 17. Liberty! Freedom! ____ is dead!

_____ 18. _____ Caesar

_____ 19. Servant to Brutus

_____ 20. Calpurnia tries to convince Caesar that her ____ are omens of tragedy

Julius Caesar Fill In The Blanks 4 Answer Key

LIGARIUS	1. Vows to follow Brutus
LEPIDUS	2. Joins with Octavius and Antony and is used by them
CASCA	3. First to stab Caesar
CINNA	4. Plants the forged letter for Cassius
DECIUS	5. Reinterprets Calpurnia's dream and convinces Caesar to go to Senate
TITINIUS	6. Officer, guards tent at Sardis
MESSALA	7. Reports Portia's death, discovers Cassius's body
BRUTUS	8. Joins and then leads the conspiracy to kill Caesar
ARTEMIDORUS	9. Gives Caesar a letter of warning naming the conspirators
MISCHIEF	10. ____, thou art afoot, Take thou what course thou wilt.
LUCILIUS	11. Captured by Antony's soldiers, mistaken for Brutus
CONSPIRACY	12. An agreement to perform together an illegal act
PINDARUS	13. Servant to Cassius
BUTCHERS	14. Let us be sacrificers, but not ____, Caius.
HUNGRY	15. Yond Cassius has a lean and ___ look.
PORTIA	16. Wife of Brutus
TYRANNY	17. Liberty! Freedom! ____ is dead!
JULIUS	18. _____ Caesar
LUCIUS	19. Servant to Brutus
DREAMS	20. Calpurnia tries to convince Caesar that her ____ are omens of tragedy

Julius Caesar Matching 1

___ 1. PUBLIUS   A. Warns Caesar to 'Beware the Ides of March'
___ 2. OATH   B. Servant to Brutus
___ 3. BRUTUS   C. Holds Brutus's suicide sword
___ 4. VARRO   D. Plants the forged letter for Cassius
___ 5. LUCIUS   E. Officer, guards tent at Sardis
___ 6. FUNERAL   F. Caesar goes to this meeting
___ 7. TITINIUS   G. Wishes Cassius well in his 'enterprise'
___ 8. FLAVIUS   H. Reinterprets Calpurnia's dream and convinces Caesar to go to Senate
___ 9. WIFE   I. Joins with Octavius and Antony and is used by them
___10. STRATO   J. Caesar's wife
___11. LUCILIUS   K. Tribune who breaks up crowd waiting to honor Caesar's triumph
___12. LEPIDUS   L. _____ Caesar
___13. CICERO   M. Help, ho! They ____ Caesar!
___14. JULIUS   N. Yond Cassius has a lean and ___ look.
___15. DREAMS   O. One of many who escort Caesar to the Senate meeting
___16. MURDER   P. Wife of Brutus
___17. CINNA   Q. Servant of Brutus
___18. MESSALA   R. Brutus thinks a just cause needs no ___ to bind the doers to their cause
___19. SOOTHSAYER   S. Reports Portia's death, discovers Cassius's body
___20. PAPILIUS   T. Roman Senator to whom Casca talks on the eve of the assassination
___21. HUNGRY   U. Captured by Antony's soldiers, mistaken for Brutus
___22. PORTIA   V. Joins and then leads the conspiracy to kill Caesar
___23. SENATE   W. Antony spoke at Caesar's
___24. DECIUS   X. Calpurnia tries to convince Caesar that her ____ are omens of tragedy
___25. CALPURNIA   Y. Render me worthy of this noble ____!

Julius Caesar Matching 1 Answer Key

O - 1. PUBLIUS	A.	Warns Caesar to 'Beware the Ides of March'
R - 2. OATH	B.	Servant to Brutus
V - 3. BRUTUS	C.	Holds Brutus's suicide sword
Q - 4. VARRO	D.	Plants the forged letter for Cassius
B - 5. LUCIUS	E.	Officer, guards tent at Sardis
W - 6. FUNERAL	F.	Caesar goes to this meeting
E - 7. TITINIUS	G.	Wishes Cassius well in his 'enterprise'
K - 8. FLAVIUS	H.	Reinterprets Calpurnia's dream and convinces Caesar to go to Senate
Y - 9. WIFE	I.	Joins with Octavius and Antony and is used by them
C - 10. STRATO	J.	Caesar's wife
U - 11. LUCILIUS	K.	Tribune who breaks up crowd waiting to honor Caesar's triumph
I - 12. LEPIDUS	L.	_____ Caesar
T - 13. CICERO	M.	Help, ho! They _____ Caesar!
L - 14. JULIUS	N.	Yond Cassius has a lean and ___ look.
X - 15. DREAMS	O.	One of many who escort Caesar to the Senate meeting
M - 16. MURDER	P.	Wife of Brutus
D - 17. CINNA	Q.	Servant of Brutus
S - 18. MESSALA	R.	Brutus thinks a just cause needs no ___ to bind the doers to their cause
A - 19. SOOTHSAYER	S.	Reports Portia's death, discovers Cassius's body
G - 20. PAPILIUS	T.	Roman Senator to whom Casca talks on the eve of the assassination
N - 21. HUNGRY	U.	Captured by Antony's soldiers, mistaken for Brutus
P - 22. PORTIA	V.	Joins and then leads the conspiracy to kill Caesar
F - 23. SENATE	W.	Antony spoke at Caesar's
H - 24. DECIUS	X.	Calpurnia tries to convince Caesar that her _____ are omens of tragedy
J - 25. CALPURNIA	Y.	Render me worthy of this noble ____!

Julius Caesar Matching 2

___ 1. DREAMS
___ 2. MAN
___ 3. CALPURNIA
___ 4. ROME
___ 5. PAPILIUS
___ 6. FUNERAL
___ 7. CROWN
___ 8. MISCHIEF
___ 9. CINNA
___ 10. METELLUS
___ 11. WIFE
___ 12. SWORD
___ 13. PUBLIUS
___ 14. FRIENDS
___ 15. CICERO
___ 16. STRATO
___ 17. TREBONIUS
___ 18. CLITUS
___ 19. BRUTUS
___ 20. ARTEMIDORUS
___ 21. VARRO
___ 22. SENATE
___ 23. ANTONY
___ 24. MESSALA
___ 25. TYRANNY

A. Servant of Brutus
B. Caesar, thou art revenged, Even with the ___ that killed thee.
C. Gives Caesar a letter of warning naming the conspirators
D. Roman Senator to whom Casca talks on the eve of the assassination
E. Distracts Caesar's attention so conspirators can carry out their plan
F. ... not that I loved Caesar less, but that I loved ___ more
G. Render me worthy of this noble ___!
H. Liberty! Freedom! ___ is dead!
I. Caesar's wife
J. Antony spoke at Caesar's
K. Antony offered Caesar one
L. Plants the forged letter for Cassius
M. Joins and then leads the conspiracy to kill Caesar
N. Calpurnia tries to convince Caesar that her ___ are omens of tragedy
O. Holds Brutus's suicide sword
P. Wishes Cassius well in his 'enterprise'
Q. ... that Nature might stand up/And say to all the world, 'This was a ___'
R. One of many who escort Caesar to the Senate meeting
S. ___, Romans, countrymen, lend me your ears.
T. Caesar goes to this meeting
U. Reports Portia's death, discovers Cassius's body
V. Servant of Brutus; refused to kill Brutus
W. Devoted follower of Caesar; defeats Brutus
X. ___, thou art afoot, Take thou what course thou wilt.
Y. Takes Antony away from the assassination scene so he won't interfere

Julius Caesar Matching 2 Answer Key

N - 1.	DREAMS	A.	Servant of Brutus
Q - 2.	MAN	B.	Caesar, thou art revenged, Even with the ___ that killed thee.
I - 3.	CALPURNIA	C.	Gives Caesar a letter of warning naming the conspirators
F - 4.	ROME	D.	Roman Senator to whom Casca talks on the eve of the assassination
P - 5.	PAPILIUS	E.	Distracts Caesar's attention so conspirators can carry out their plan
J - 6.	FUNERAL	F.	... not that I loved Caesar less, but that I loved ___ more
K - 7.	CROWN	G.	Render me worthy of this noble ___!
X - 8.	MISCHIEF	H.	Liberty! Freedom! ___ is dead!
L - 9.	CINNA	I.	Caesar's wife
E -10.	METELLUS	J.	Antony spoke at Caesar's
G -11.	WIFE	K.	Antony offered Caesar one
B -12.	SWORD	L.	Plants the forged letter for Cassius
R -13.	PUBLIUS	M.	Joins and then leads the conspiracy to kill Caesar
S -14.	FRIENDS	N.	Calpurnia tries to convince Caesar that her ___ are omens of tragedy
D -15.	CICERO	O.	Holds Brutus's suicide sword
O -16.	STRATO	P.	Wishes Cassius well in his 'enterprise'
Y -17.	TREBONIUS	Q.	... that Nature might stand up/And say to all the world, 'This was a ___'
V -18.	CLITUS	R.	One of many who escort Caesar to the Senate meeting
M -19.	BRUTUS	S.	___, Romans, countrymen, lend me your ears.
C -20.	ARTEMIDORUS	T.	Caesar goes to this meeting
A -21.	VARRO	U.	Reports Portia's death, discovers Cassius's body
T -22.	SENATE	V.	Servant of Brutus; refused to kill Brutus
W -23.	ANTONY	W.	Devoted follower of Caesar; defeats Brutus
U -24.	MESSALA	X.	___, thou art afoot, Take thou what course thou wilt.
H -25.	TYRANNY	Y.	Takes Antony away from the assassination scene so he won't interfere

Julius Caesar Matching 3

___ 1. WIFE
___ 2. PINDARUS
___ 3. TYRANNY
___ 4. MISCHIEF
___ 5. CASCA
___ 6. ANTONY
___ 7. CINNA
___ 8. DREAMS
___ 9. MARCH
___ 10. LUCIUS
___ 11. LUCILIUS
___ 12. SWORD
___ 13. CALPURNIA
___ 14. VARRO
___ 15. PAPILIUS
___ 16. CASSIUS
___ 17. ROME
___ 18. PORTIA
___ 19. MESSALA
___ 20. LIGARIUS
___ 21. FUNERAL
___ 22. BUTCHERS
___ 23. SOOTHSAYER
___ 24. MAN
___ 25. LEPIDUS

A. Servant to Brutus
B. Caesar's wife
C. Let us be sacrificers, but not ____, Caius.
D. ... not that I loved Caesar less, but that I loved ___ more
E. ... that Nature might stand up/And say to all the world, 'This was a ___'
F. Render me worthy of this noble ____!
G. Liberty! Freedom! ____ is dead!
H. Caesar, thou art revenged, Even with the ___ that killed thee.
I. Reports Portia's death, discovers Cassius's body
J. ____, thou art afoot, Take thou what course thou wilt.
K. Devoted follower of Caesar; defeats Brutus
L. Joins with Octavius and Antony and is used by them
M. Servant to Cassius
N. Wishes Cassius well in his 'enterprise'
O. Organizes the conspiracy & gets Brutus to join
P. Vows to follow Brutus
Q. Calpurnia tries to convince Caesar that her ____ are omens of tragedy
R. Wife of Brutus
S. First to stab Caesar
T. Warns Caesar to 'Beware the Ides of March'
U. Captured by Antony's soldiers, mistaken for Brutus
V. Antony spoke at Caesar's
W. Plants the forged letter for Cassius
X. Beware the Ides of ___
Y. Servant of Brutus

Julius Caesar Matching 3 Answer Key

F - 1. WIFE
M - 2. PINDARUS
G - 3. TYRANNY
J - 4. MISCHIEF
S - 5. CASCA
K - 6. ANTONY
W - 7. CINNA
Q - 8. DREAMS
X - 9. MARCH
A - 10. LUCIUS
U - 11. LUCILIUS
H - 12. SWORD
B - 13. CALPURNIA
Y - 14. VARRO
N - 15. PAPILIUS
O - 16. CASSIUS
D - 17. ROME
R - 18. PORTIA
I - 19. MESSALA
P - 20. LIGARIUS
V - 21. FUNERAL
C - 22. BUTCHERS
T - 23. SOOTHSAYER
E - 24. MAN
L - 25. LEPIDUS

A. Servant to Brutus
B. Caesar's wife
C. Let us be sacrificers, but not ____, Caius.
D. ... not that I loved Caesar less, but that I loved ___ more
E. ... that Nature might stand up/And say to all the world, 'This was a ___'
F. Render me worthy of this noble ____!
G. Liberty! Freedom! ____ is dead!
H. Caesar, thou art revenged, Even with the ___ that killed thee.
I. Reports Portia's death, discovers Cassius's body
J. ____, thou art afoot, Take thou what course thou wilt.
K. Devoted follower of Caesar; defeats Brutus
L. Joins with Octavius and Antony and is used by them
M. Servant to Cassius
N. Wishes Cassius well in his 'enterprise'
O. Organizes the conspiracy & gets Brutus to join
P. Vows to follow Brutus
Q. Calpurnia tries to convince Caesar that her ____ are omens of tragedy
R. Wife of Brutus
S. First to stab Caesar
T. Warns Caesar to 'Beware the Ides of March'
U. Captured by Antony's soldiers, mistaken for Brutus
V. Antony spoke at Caesar's
W. Plants the forged letter for Cassius
X. Beware the Ides of ___
Y. Servant of Brutus

Julius Caesar Matching 4

___ 1. CALPURNIA
___ 2. CROWN
___ 3. PINDARUS
___ 4. CATO
___ 5. CASCA
___ 6. SWORD
___ 7. PAPILIUS
___ 8. FLAVIUS
___ 9. TYRANNY
___ 10. MIGHTY
___ 11. FUNERAL
___ 12. WILL
___ 13. CONSPIRACY
___ 14. MURDER
___ 15. STRATO
___ 16. JULIUS
___ 17. MISCHIEF
___ 18. MESSALA
___ 19. SENATE
___ 20. PORTIA
___ 21. TREBONIUS
___ 22. PUBLIUS
___ 23. VARRO
___ 24. OCTAVIUS
___ 25. HUNGRY

A. Caesar goes to this meeting
B. One of many who escort Caesar to the Senate meeting
C. Wishes Cassius well in his 'enterprise'
D. Antony offered Caesar one
E. Soldier in army of Brutus & Cassius
F. ____, thou art afoot, Take thou what course thou wilt.
G. Servant to Cassius
H. Tribune who breaks up crowd waiting to honor Caesar's triumph
I. Antony spoke at Caesar's
J. Caesar's wife
K. Caesar, thou art revenged, Even with the ___ that killed thee.
L. Reports Portia's death, discovers Cassius's body
M. Yond Cassius has a lean and ___ look.
N. O Julius Caesar, thou art ____ yet.
O. First to stab Caesar
P. Wife of Brutus
Q. _____ Caesar
R. Servant of Brutus
S. Liberty! Freedom! ____ is dead!
T. Caesar, now be still. I killed not thee with half so good a ____.
U. Heir of Julius Caesar
V. Help, ho! They ____ Caesar!
W. Takes Antony away from the assassination scene so he won't interfere
X. An agreement to perform together an illegal act
Y. Holds Brutus's suicide sword

Julius Caesar Matching 4 Answer Key

J - 1.	CALPURNIA	A.	Caesar goes to this meeting
D - 2.	CROWN	B.	One of many who escort Caesar to the Senate meeting
G - 3.	PINDARUS	C.	Wishes Cassius well in his 'enterprise'
E - 4.	CATO	D.	Antony offered Caesar one
O - 5.	CASCA	E.	Soldier in army of Brutus & Cassius
K - 6.	SWORD	F.	____, thou art afoot, Take thou what course thou wilt.
C - 7.	PAPILIUS	G.	Servant to Cassius
H - 8.	FLAVIUS	H.	Tribune who breaks up crowd waiting to honor Caesar's triumph
S - 9.	TYRANNY	I.	Antony spoke at Caesar's
N -10.	MIGHTY	J.	Caesar's wife
I - 11.	FUNERAL	K.	Caesar, thou art revenged, Even with the ___ that killed thee.
T -12.	WILL	L.	Reports Portia's death, discovers Cassius's body
X -13.	CONSPIRACY	M.	Yond Cassius has a lean and ___ look.
V -14.	MURDER	N.	O Julius Caesar, thou art ____ yet.
Y -15.	STRATO	O.	First to stab Caesar
Q -16.	JULIUS	P.	Wife of Brutus
F -17.	MISCHIEF	Q.	_____ Caesar
L -18.	MESSALA	R.	Servant of Brutus
A -19.	SENATE	S.	Liberty! Freedom! ____ is dead!
P -20.	PORTIA	T.	Caesar, now be still. I killed not thee with half so good a ____.
W -21.	TREBONIUS	U.	Heir of Julius Caesar
B -22.	PUBLIUS	V.	Help, ho! They ____ Caesar!
R -23.	VARRO	W.	Takes Antony away from the assassination scene so he won't interfere
U -24.	OCTAVIUS	X.	An agreement to perform together an illegal act
M -25.	HUNGRY	Y.	Holds Brutus's suicide sword

Julius Caesar Magic Squares 1

Match the definition with the vocabulary word. Put your answers in the magic squares below. When your answers are correct, all columns and rows will add to the same number.

A. CROWN
B. PINDARUS
C. FUNERAL
D. CICERO
E. CALPURNIA
F. BRUTUS
G. WILL
H. CLITUS
I. ROME
J. VARRO
K. LUCIUS
L. DREAMS
M. SENATE
N. PORTIA
O. BUTCHERS
P. CATO

1. Servant of Brutus; refused to kill Brutus
2. Caesar goes to this meeting
3. Servant to Cassius
4. Servant to Brutus
5. Servant of Brutus
6. Antony spoke at Caesar's
7. Soldier in army of Brutus & Cassius
8. Caesar's wife
9. Let us be sacrificers, but not ____, Caius.
10. Joins and then leads the conspiracy to kill Caesar
11. ... not that I loved Caesar less, but that I loved ____ more
12. Roman Senator to whom Casca talks on the eve of the assassination
13. Antony offered Caesar one
14. Calpurnia tries to convince Caesar that her ____ are omens of tragedy
15. Caesar, now be still. I killed not thee with half so good a ____.
16. Wife of Brutus

A=	B=	C=	D=
E=	F=	G=	H=
I=	J=	K=	L=
M=	N=	O=	P=

Julius Caesar Magic Squares 1 Answer Key

Match the definition with the vocabulary word. Put your answers in the magic squares below. When your answers are correct, all columns and rows will add to the same number.

A. CROWN
B. PINDARUS
C. FUNERAL
D. CICERO
E. CALPURNIA
F. BRUTUS
G. WILL
H. CLITUS
I. ROME
J. VARRO
K. LUCIUS
L. DREAMS
M. SENATE
N. PORTIA
O. BUTCHERS
P. CATO

1. Servant of Brutus; refused to kill Brutus
2. Caesar goes to this meeting
3. Servant to Cassius
4. Servant to Brutus
5. Servant of Brutus
6. Antony spoke at Caesar's
7. Soldier in army of Brutus & Cassius
8. Caesar's wife
9. Let us be sacrificers, but not ____, Caius.
10. Joins and then leads the conspiracy to kill Caesar
11. ... not that I loved Caesar less, but that I loved ___ more
12. Roman Senator to whom Casca talks on the eve of the assassination
13. Antony offered Caesar one
14. Calpurnia tries to convince Caesar that her ____ are omens of tragedy
15. Caesar, now be still. I killed not thee with half so good a ____.
16. Wife of Brutus

A=13	B=3	C=6	D=12
E=8	F=10	G=15	H=1
I=11	J=5	K=4	L=14
M=2	N=16	O=9	P=7

Julius Caesar Magic Squares 2

Match the definition with the vocabulary word. Put your answers in the magic squares below. When your answers are correct, all columns and rows will add to the same number.

A. SWORD
B. LUCILIUS
C. CATO
D. BUTCHERS
E. CINNA
F. SENATE
G. MAN
H. MARCH
I. LUCIUS
J. MURDER
K. FUNERAL
L. CALPURNIA
M. CICERO
N. CONSPIRACY
O. TYRANNY
P. SOOTHSAYER

1. Beware the Ides of ___
2. Caesar, thou art revenged, Even with the ___ that killed thee.
3. Captured by Antony's soldiers, mistaken for Brutus
4. ... that Nature might stand up/And say to all the world, 'This was a ___'
5. Help, ho! They ___ Caesar!
6. Liberty! Freedom! ___ is dead!
7. Warns Caesar to 'Beware the Ides of March'
8. Servant to Brutus
9. Antony spoke at Caesar's ___
10. An agreement to perform together an illegal act
11. Roman Senator to whom Casca talks on the eve of the assassination
12. Caesar's wife
13. Plants the forged letter for Cassius
14. Let us be sacrificers, but not ___, Caius.
15. Soldier in army of Brutus & Cassius
16. Caesar goes to this meeting

A=	B=	C=	D=
E=	F=	G=	H=
I=	J=	K=	L=
M=	N=	O=	P=

Julius Caesar Magic Squares 2 Answer Key

Match the definition with the vocabulary word. Put your answers in the magic squares below. When your answers are correct, all columns and rows will add to the same number.

A. SWORD
B. LUCILIUS
C. CATO
D. BUTCHERS
E. CINNA
F. SENATE
G. MAN
H. MARCH
I. LUCIUS
J. MURDER
K. FUNERAL
L. CALPURNIA
M. CICERO
N. CONSPIRACY
O. TYRANNY
P. SOOTHSAYER

1. Beware the Ides of ___
2. Caesar, thou art revenged, Even with the ___ that killed thee.
3. Captured by Antony's soldiers, mistaken for Brutus
4. ... that Nature might stand up/And say to all the world, 'This was a ___'
5. Help, ho! They ____ Caesar!
6. Liberty! Freedom! ____ is dead!
7. Warns Caesar to 'Beware the Ides of March'
8. Servant to Brutus
9. Antony spoke at Caesar's ___
10. An agreement to perform together an illegal act
11. Roman Senator to whom Casca talks on the eve of the assassination
12. Caesar's wife
13. Plants the forged letter for Cassius
14. Let us be sacrificers, but not ____, Caius.
15. Soldier in army of Brutus & Cassius
16. Caesar goes to this meeting

A=2	B=3	C=15	D=14
E=13	F=16	G=4	H=1
I=8	J=5	K=9	L=12
M=11	N=10	O=6	P=7

Julius Caesar Magic Squares 3

Match the definition with the vocabulary word. Put your answers in the magic squares below. When your answers are correct, all columns and rows will add to the same number.

A. MARCH
B. OCTAVIUS
C. CASCA
D. MAN
E. MIGHT
F. CICERO
G. METELLUS
H. BUTCHERS
I. CONSPIRACY
J. HUNGRY
K. CASSIUS
L. BRUTUS
M. JULIUS
N. LEPIDUS
O. SENATE
P. SWORD

1. Caesar goes to this meeting
2. Yond Cassius has a lean and ___ look.
3. Let us be sacrificers, but not ___, Caius.
4. Beware the Ides of ___
5. ... that Nature might stand up/And say to all the world, 'This was a ___'
6. I have a man's mind, but a woman's ___.
7. Organizes the conspiracy & gets Brutus to join
8. Joins with Octavius and Antony and is used by them
9. Roman Senator to whom Casca talks on the eve of the assassination
10. First to stab Caesar
11. _____ Caesar
12. Joins and then leads the conspiracy to kill Caesar
13. An agreement to perform together an illegal act
14. Caesar, thou art revenged, Even with the ___ that killed thee.
15. Heir of Julius Caesar
16. Distracts Caesar's attention so conspirators can carry out their plan

A=	B=	C=	D=
E=	F=	G=	H=
I=	J=	K=	L=
M=	N=	O=	P=

Julius Caesar Magic Squares 3 Answer Key

Match the definition with the vocabulary word. Put your answers in the magic squares below. When your answers are correct, all columns and rows will add to the same number.

A. MARCH
B. OCTAVIUS
C. CASCA
D. MAN
E. MIGHT
F. CICERO
G. METELLUS
H. BUTCHERS
I. CONSPIRACY
J. HUNGRY
K. CASSIUS
L. BRUTUS
M. JULIUS
N. LEPIDUS
O. SENATE
P. SWORD

1. Caesar goes to this meeting
2. Yond Cassius has a lean and ___ look.
3. Let us be sacrificers, but not ___, Caius.
4. Beware the Ides of ___
5. ... that Nature might stand up/And say to all the world, 'This was a ___'
6. I have a man's mind, but a woman's ___.
7. Organizes the conspiracy & gets Brutus to join
8. Joins with Octavius and Antony and is used by them
9. Roman Senator to whom Casca talks on the eve of the assassination
10. First to stab Caesar
11. _____ Caesar
12. Joins and then leads the conspiracy to kill Caesar
13. An agreement to perform together an illegal act
14. Caesar, thou art revenged, Even with the ___ that killed thee.
15. Heir of Julius Caesar
16. Distracts Caesar's attention so conspirators can carry out their plan

A=4	B=15	C=10	D=5
E=6	F=9	G=16	H=3
I=13	J=2	K=7	L=12
M=11	N=8	O=1	P=14

Julius Caesar Magic Squares 4

Match the definition with the vocabulary word. Put your answers in the magic squares below. When your answers are correct, all columns and rows will add to the same number.

A. SOOTHSAYER
B. CONSPIRACY
C. MURDER
D. MARCH
E. VARRO
F. PUBLIUS
G. TYRANNY
H. JULIUS
I. ARTEMIDORUS
J. SENATE
K. CICERO
L. FRIENDS
M. TREBONIUS
N. LEPIDUS
O. MISCHIEF
P. DECIUS

1. Help, ho! They ____ Caesar!
2. Caesar goes to this meeting
3. One of many who escort Caesar to the Senate meeting
4. ____, thou art afoot, Take thou what course thou wilt.
5. Reinterprets Calpurnia's dream and convinces Caesar to go to Senate
6. Servant of Brutus
7. Gives Caesar a letter of warning naming the conspirators
8. Beware the Ides of ___
9. Takes Antony away from the assassination scene so he won't interfere
10. _____ Caesar
11. ____, Romans, countrymen, lend me your ears.
12. Warns Caesar to 'Beware the Ides of March'
13. An agreement to perform together an illegal act
14. Roman Senator to whom Casca talks on the eve of the assassination
15. Liberty! Freedom! ____ is dead!
16. Joins with Octavius and Antony and is used by them

A=	B=	C=	D=
E=	F=	G=	H=
I=	J=	K=	L=
M=	N=	O=	P=

Julius Caesar Magic Squares 4 Answer Key

Match the definition with the vocabulary word. Put your answers in the magic squares below. When your answers are correct, all columns and rows will add to the same number.

A. SOOTHSAYER
B. CONSPIRACY
C. MURDER
D. MARCH
E. VARRO
F. PUBLIUS
G. TYRANNY
H. JULIUS
I. ARTEMIDORUS
J. SENATE
K. CICERO
L. FRIENDS
M. TREBONIUS
N. LEPIDUS
O. MISCHIEF
P. DECIUS

1. Help, ho! They ____ Caesar!
2. Caesar goes to this meeting
3. One of many who escort Caesar to the Senate meeting
4. ____, thou art afoot, Take thou what course thou wilt.
5. Reinterprets Calpurnia's dream and convinces Caesar to go to Senate
6. Servant of Brutus
7. Gives Caesar a letter of warning naming the conspirators
8. Beware the Ides of ___
9. Takes Antony away from the assassination scene so he won't interfere
10. _____ Caesar
11. ____, Romans, countrymen, lend me your ears.
12. Warns Caesar to 'Beware the Ides of March'
13. An agreement to perform together an illegal act
14. Roman Senator to whom Casca talks on the eve of the assassination
15. Liberty! Freedom! ____ is dead!
16. Joins with Octavius and Antony and is used by them

A=12	B=13	C=1	D=8
E=6	F=3	G=15	H=10
I=7	J=2	K=14	L=11
M=9	N=16	O=4	P=5

Julius Caesar Word Search 1

```
C A R T E M I D O R U S M D P E B D C Z
R L H Y W T O C A M U V I M T W F A K
D T I M D R Y N O I F I W O G V F X S L
N R S T R A T O R N J L R B J H E P S P
N E E A U O J A M B S I P G S T T S I V
K B V A N S G D M H M P R K A B F Y U Z
K O R Y M I T S Y O E A I N J Q F K S Z
J N W F L S Y V C P T P E R P S L S D Z
U I Y L N K R T Q O E S M F A R Z U E T
L U L A D G A Z H R L R W P R C G R C G
I S C V X V N K M T L Y M J M I Y A I H
U J M I I Q N D Y I U S J U A X E D U L
S U T U R B Y T C A S C A C R O W N S Z
C Y S S F S B I M U M C I G C D G I D M
O A R T H D C Q I M M N H D H R E P L S
A N T H W E K C G M N H M I Y F F R F L
T S Z O R P U J H A L A S S E M I Z N W
H Q Y O K L V S T N S W O R D F W X R Y
```

... not that I loved Caesar less, but that I loved ___ more (4)
... that Nature might stand up/And say to all the world, 'This was a ___' (3)
An agreement to perform together an illegal act (10)
Antony offered Caesar one (5)
Beware the Ides of ___ (5)
Brutus thinks a just cause needs no ___ to bind the doers to their cause (4)
Caesar goes to this meeting (6)
Caesar, now be still. I killed not thee with half so good a ____. (4)
Caesar, thou art revenged, Even with the ___ that killed thee. (5)
Calpurnia tries to convince Caesar that her ____ are omens of tragedy (6)
Devoted follower of Caesar; defeats Brutus (6)
Distracts Caesar's attention so conspirators can carry out their plan (8)
First to stab Caesar (5)
Gives Caesar a letter of warning naming the conspirators (11)
Heir of Julius Caesar (8)
Help, ho! They ____ Caesar! (6)
Holds Brutus's suicide sword (6)
I have a man's mind, but a woman's ____. (5)
Joins and then leads the conspiracy to kill Caesar (6)
Liberty! Freedom! ____ is dead! (7)

O Julius Caesar, thou art ____ yet. (6)
Organizes the conspiracy & gets Brutus to join (7)
Plants the forged letter for Cassius (5)
Reinterprets Calpurnia's dream and convinces Caesar to go to Senate (6)
Render me worthy of this noble ____! (4)
Reports Portia's death, discovers Cassius's body (7)
Roman Senator to whom Casca talks on the eve of the assassination (6)
Servant of Brutus (5)
Servant of Brutus; refused to kill Brutus (6)
Servant to Brutus (6)
Servant to Cassius (8)
Soldier in army of Brutus & Cassius (4)
Takes Antony away from the assassination scene so he won't interfere (9)
Tribune who breaks up crowd waiting to honor Caesar's triumph (7)
Vows to follow Brutus (8)
Wife of Brutus (6)
Wishes Cassius well in his 'enterprise' (8)
Yond Cassius has a lean and ___ look. (6)
____, Romans, countrymen, lend me your ears. (7)
____, thou art afoot, Take thou what course thou wilt. (8)
_____ Caesar (6)

Julius Caesar Word Search 1 Answer Key

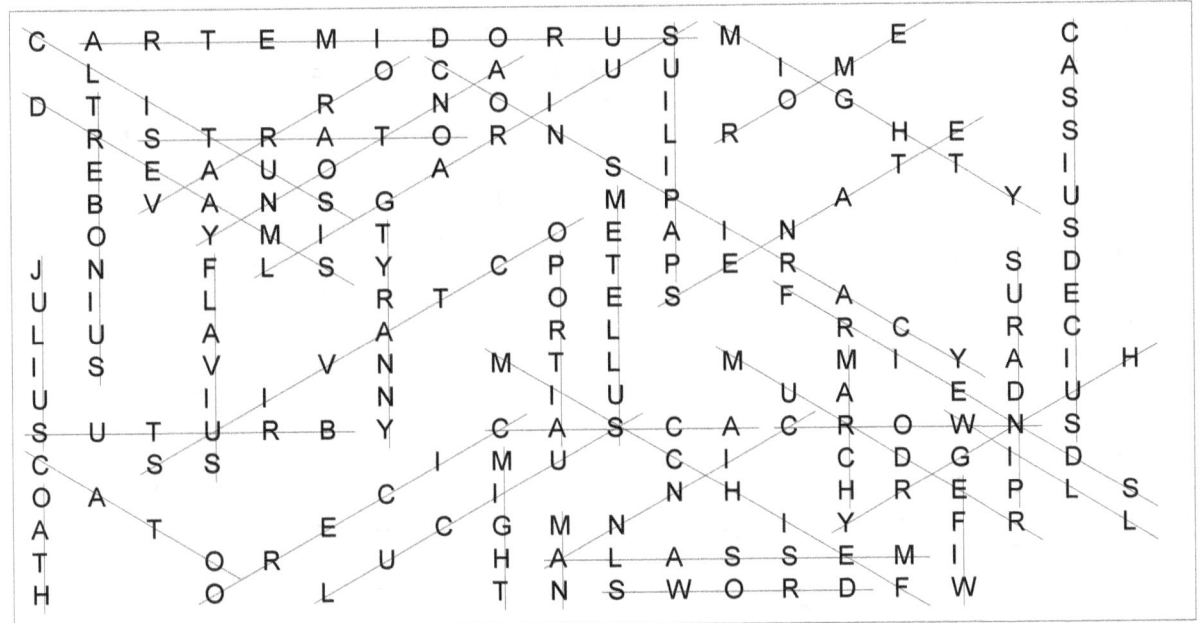

- ... not that I loved Caesar less, but that I loved ___ more (4)
- ... that Nature might stand up/And say to all the world, 'This was a ___' (3)
- An agreement to perform together an illegal act (10)
- Antony offered Caesar one (5)
- Beware the Ides of ___ (5)
- Brutus thinks a just cause needs no ___ to bind the doers to their cause (4)
- Caesar goes to this meeting (6)
- Caesar, now be still. I killed not thee with half so good a ____. (4)
- Caesar, thou art revenged, Even with the ___ that killed thee. (5)
- Calpurnia tries to convince Caesar that her ____ are omens of tragedy (6)
- Devoted follower of Caesar; defeats Brutus (6)
- Distracts Caesar's attention so conspirators can carry out their plan (8)
- First to stab Caesar (5)
- Gives Caesar a letter of warning naming the conspirators (11)
- Heir of Julius Caesar (8)
- Help, ho! They ____ Caesar! (6)
- Holds Brutus's suicide sword (6)
- I have a man's mind, but a woman's ____. (5)
- Joins and then leads the conspiracy to kill Caesar (6)
- Liberty! Freedom! ____ is dead! (7)
- O Julius Caesar, thou art ____ yet. (6)
- Organizes the conspiracy & gets Brutus to join (7)
- Plants the forged letter for Cassius (5)
- Reinterprets Calpurnia's dream and convinces Caesar to go to Senate (6)
- Render me worthy of this noble ____! (4)
- Reports Portia's death, discovers Cassius's body (7)
- Roman Senator to whom Casca talks on the eve of the assassination (6)
- Servant of Brutus (5)
- Servant of Brutus; refused to kill Brutus (6)
- Servant to Brutus (6)
- Servant to Cassius (8)
- Soldier in army of Brutus & Cassius (4)
- Takes Antony away from the assassination scene so he won't interfere (9)
- Tribune who breaks up crowd waiting to honor Caesar's triumph (7)
- Vows to follow Brutus (8)
- Wife of Brutus (6)
- Wishes Cassius well in his 'enterprise' (8)
- Yond Cassius has a lean and ___ look. (6)
- ____, Romans, countrymen, lend me your ears. (7)
- ____, thou art afoot, Take thou what course thou wilt. (8)
- _____ Caesar (6)

Julius Caesar Word Search 2

```
C A L P U R N I A R F T C C A S S I U S
P R J U L I U S T P S E N A T E U M Q C
F I O K S Z F F L Y B Q S Y T J I I Q M
V W N W C V J R U T R P J W Z O N G O V
F F L D N A N I C R C A P M I F M H A W
T L N G A R D E I Y S J N A U L U T T P
Z A T X Y R G N U H B S S N R C L Y H S
N V Q D E O U D S K U R E P Y I O M A N
W I X A J N N S M I E R W T G N V C Y O
J U M H S S H F L H A D W A R N S N C P
L S U T U R B B C L G P R F J A O T S P
M E X N I F U T I H W I A O C T A U W J
U R P T C P U W C T U M T P N V T J O T
R S O I E B I M E S S A L A I I K T R Z
D G R M D F Z K R M R B U L L H R D T
E H T D E U G W O T J C S C N G I W V M
R M I N V G S C S S H J T I R S U J G
X R A L R L D S U R O D I M E T R A S L
```

... not that I loved Caesar less, but that I loved ___ more (4)
... that Nature might stand up/And say to all the world, 'This was a ___' (3)
Antony offered Caesar one (5)
Antony spoke at Caesar's (7)
Beware the Ides of ___ (5)
Brutus thinks a just cause needs no ___ to bind the doers to their cause (4)
Caesar goes to this meeting (6)
Caesar's wife (9)
Caesar, now be still. I killed not thee with half so good a ____. (4)
Caesar, thou art revenged, Even with the ___ that killed thee. (5)
Calpurnia tries to convince Caesar that her ____ are omens of tragedy (6)
Devoted follower of Caesar; defeats Brutus (6)
First to stab Caesar (5)
Friend & soldier to Brutus; refuses to hold Brutus's sword (9)
Gives Caesar a letter of warning naming the conspirators (11)
Heir of Julius Caesar (8)
Help, ho! They ____ Caesar! (6)
Holds Brutus's suicide sword (6)
I have a man's mind, but a woman's ____. (5)
Joins and then leads the conspiracy to kill Caesar (6)
Joins with Octavius and Antony and is used by them (7)
Let us be sacrificers, but not ____, Caius. (8)
Liberty! Freedom! ____ is dead! (7)
O Julius Caesar, thou art ____ yet. (6)
One of many who escort Caesar to the Senate meeting (7)
Organizes the conspiracy & gets Brutus to join (7)
Plants the forged letter for Cassius (5)
Reinterprets Calpurnia's dream and convinces Caesar to go to Senate (6)
Render me worthy of this noble ____! (4)
Reports Portia's death, discovers Cassius's body (7)
Roman Senator to whom Casca talks on the eve of the assassination (6)
Servant of Brutus (5)
Servant of Brutus; refused to kill Brutus (6)
Servant to Brutus (6)
Servant to Cassius (8)
Soldier in army of Brutus & Cassius (4)
Tribune who breaks up crowd waiting to honor Caesar's triumph (7)
Vows to follow Brutus (8)
Wife of Brutus (6)
Wishes Cassius well in his 'enterprise' (8)
Yond Cassius has a lean and ___ look. (6)
____, Romans, countrymen, lend me your ears. (7)
_____ Caesar (6)

Julius Caesar Word Search 2 Answer Key

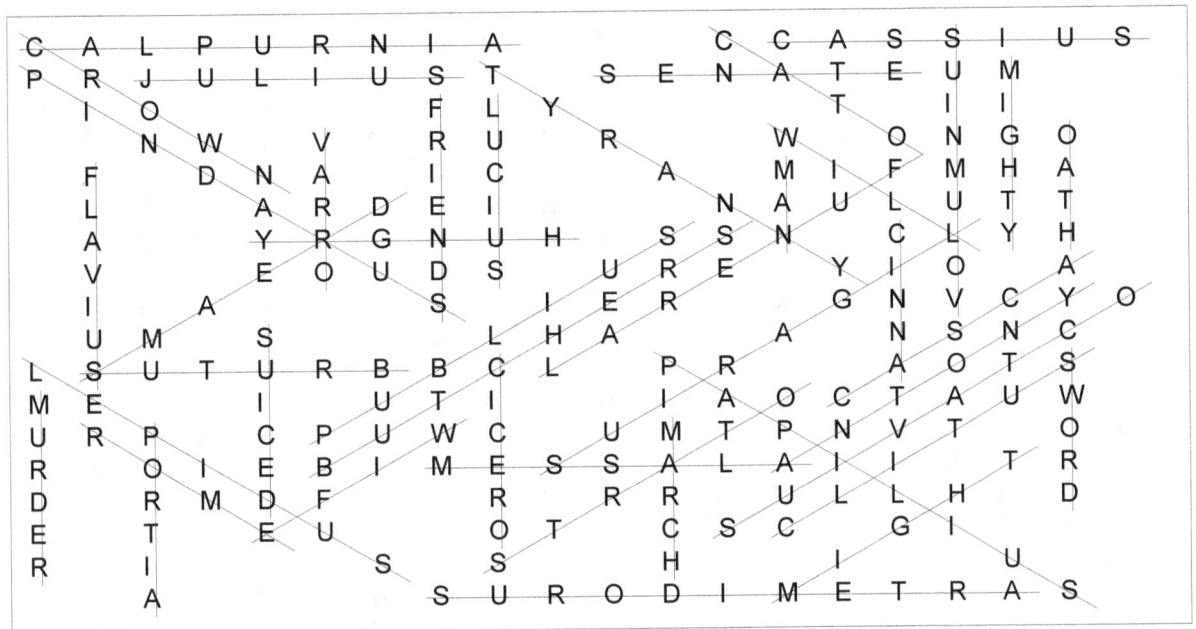

- ... not that I loved Caesar less, but that I loved ___ more (4)
- ... that Nature might stand up/And say to all the world, 'This was a ___' (3)
- Antony offered Caesar one (5)
- Antony spoke at Caesar's (7)
- Beware the Ides of ___ (5)
- Brutus thinks a just cause needs no ___ to bind the doers to their cause (4)
- Caesar goes to this meeting (6)
- Caesar's wife (9)
- Caesar, now be still. I killed not thee with half so good a ___. (4)
- Caesar, thou art revenged, Even with the ___ that killed thee. (5)
- Calpurnia tries to convince Caesar that her ___ are omens of tragedy (6)
- Devoted follower of Caesar; defeats Brutus (6)
- First to stab Caesar (5)
- Friend & soldier to Brutus; refuses to hold Brutus's sword (9)
- Gives Caesar a letter of warning naming the conspirators (11)
- Heir of Julius Caesar (8)
- Help, ho! They ___ Caesar! (6)
- Holds Brutus's suicide sword (6)
- I have a man's mind, but a woman's ___. (5)
- Joins and then leads the conspiracy to kill Caesar (6)
- Joins with Octavius and Antony and is used by them (7)
- Let us be sacrificers, but not ___, Caius. (8)
- Liberty! Freedom! ___ is dead! (7)
- O Julius Caesar, thou art ___ yet. (6)
- One of many who escort Caesar to the Senate meeting (7)
- Organizes the conspiracy & gets Brutus to join (7)
- Plants the forged letter for Cassius (5)
- Reinterprets Calpurnia's dream and convinces Caesar to go to Senate (6)
- Render me worthy of this noble ___! (4)
- Reports Portia's death, discovers Cassius's body (7)
- Roman Senator to whom Casca talks on the eve of the assassination (6)
- Servant of Brutus (5)
- Servant of Brutus; refused to kill Brutus (6)
- Servant to Brutus (6)
- Servant to Cassius (8)
- Soldier in army of Brutus & Cassius (4)
- Tribune who breaks up crowd waiting to honor Caesar's triumph (7)
- Vows to follow Brutus (8)
- Wife of Brutus (6)
- Wishes Cassius well in his 'enterprise' (8)
- Yond Cassius has a lean and ___ look. (6)
- ___, Romans, countrymen, lend me your ears. (7)
- ___ Caesar (6)

Julius Caesar Word Search 3

```
P V A S O O T H S A Y E R S W O R D F X
L O A N E R Y R G N H P V T T S V R H
C S R R T N R Y G N U E D E R C O I M
T R C T R O A C C I M R Y D L R L F
I E O J I O N T C C E S S D U S U N
T H N W R N Y M E R B N S F C Z N D X
I C S G N N M D T A Q M J A S R S Q
N T P S U D I P E L S V Q I C L V M B
I U I K F X Z M P J V T H S H A U P
U B R S B L I M I B M B R U D C Q S P
S M A E R O D E X X G R M A S A H T C
L N C M O T H G L N H U H L T T R I R
U V Y R E L L F C L I T U S K O W S C T
C D U L X G S U Y G A U Y Y M R B E X
I S L W S U M K C O L S Z E L P I D F
U U K Y I R M C S I M J W N H C M R S D
S U I L I P A P J U L I U S U I V A L F
S P B Y N S R H Q L F I G D B C D G N R
S U F L C W C P I E Z K U H R Y M I K N
P W F A W N H W Y F N Q K S T N S L K B
```

ANTONY   DECIUS   MESSALA   SENATE
ARTEMIDORUS   DREAMS   METELLUS   SOOTHSAYER
BRUTUS   FLAVIUS   MIGHT   STRATO
BUTCHERS   FRIENDS   MIGHTY   SWORD
CASCA   HUNGRY   MISCHIEF   TITINIUS
CASSIUS   JULIUS   MURDER   TYRANNY
CATO   LEPIDUS   OATH   VARRO
CICERO   LIGARIUS   OCTAVIUS   VOLUMNIUS
CINNA   LUCILIUS   PAPILIUS   WIFE
CLITUS   LUCIUS   PORTIA   WILL
CONSPIRACY   MAN   PUBLIUS
CROWN   MARCH   ROME

Julius Caesar Word Search 3 Answer Key

ANTONY	DECIUS	MESSALA	SENATE
ARTEMIDORUS	DREAMS	METELLUS	SOOTHSAYER
BRUTUS	FLAVIUS	MIGHT	STRATO
BUTCHERS	FRIENDS	MIGHTY	SWORD
CASCA	HUNGRY	MISCHIEF	TITINIUS
CASSIUS	JULIUS	MURDER	TYRANNY
CATO	LEPIDUS	OATH	VARRO
CICERO	LIGARIUS	OCTAVIUS	VOLUMNIUS
CINNA	LUCILIUS	PAPILIUS	WIFE
CLITUS	LUCIUS	PORTIA	WILL
CONSPIRACY	MAN	PUBLIUS	
CROWN	MARCH	ROME	

Julius Caesar Word Search 4

```
C O N S P I R A C Y S U I N O B E R T S
T Y R A N N Y L F G F B Y H M R C I T F
T T V L I G A R I U S M K P Q I D N T K
B P O H W Q Q Y T N S C B I D S A C I K
K R L D R L R W U E E I Y N B C N G N W
M P U W P O N I S R N N T D C H T P I X
H A M T S P M F M A A N C A Y I O Y U P
G W N M U R D E R L T A F R I E N D S B
C X I K I S S H J H E V G U O F Y U M W
H V U L V S F A G O S N J S S W L L A P
D F S Z A V M I C B U K S L R L N H E N
P V H L L L M T K H I H K H E S W O R D
U A A T F T A R S G S C G T H P B T D C
B R P C W V L O P H S Y E A C G I Z Q M
L R N I I Y R P Q C A M L O T R J D W S
I O K U L C T V T A C I U C U B E H U B
U C S H L I E W D S B G C Z B C C I Z S
S A B X K Z U R J C P H I N I R L T J D
S T R A T O C S O A W T U U A U M F S X
Y O C A L P U R N I A Y S M J L B B Z Y
```

ANTONY	CONSPIRACY	LIGARIUS	OATH	TITINIUS
BRUTUS	CROWN	LUCIUS	OCTAVIUS	TREBONIUS
BUTCHERS	DECIUS	MAN	PAPILIUS	TYRANNY
CALPURNIA	DREAMS	MARCH	PINDARUS	VARRO
CASCA	FLAVIUS	MESSALA	PORTIA	VOLUMNIUS
CASSIUS	FRIENDS	METELLUS	PUBLIUS	WIFE
CATO	FUNERAL	MIGHT	ROME	WILL
CICERO	HUNGRY	MIGHTY	SENATE	
CINNA	JULIUS	MISCHIEF	STRATO	
CLITUS	LEPIDUS	MURDER	SWORD	

Julius Caesar Word Search 4 Answer Key

ANTONY	CONSPIRACY	LIGARIUS	OATH	TITINIUS
BRUTUS	CROWN	LUCIUS	OCTAVIUS	TREBONIUS
BUTCHERS	DECIUS	MAN	PAPILIUS	TYRANNY
CALPURNIA	DREAMS	MARCH	PINDARUS	VARRO
CASCA	FLAVIUS	MESSALA	PORTIA	VOLUMNIUS
CASSIUS	FRIENDS	METELLUS	PUBLIUS	WIFE
CATO	FUNERAL	MIGHT	ROME	WILL
CICERO	HUNGRY	MIGHTY	SENATE	
CINNA	JULIUS	MISCHIEF	STRATO	
CLITUS	LEPIDUS	MURDER	SWORD	

Julius Caesar Crossword 1

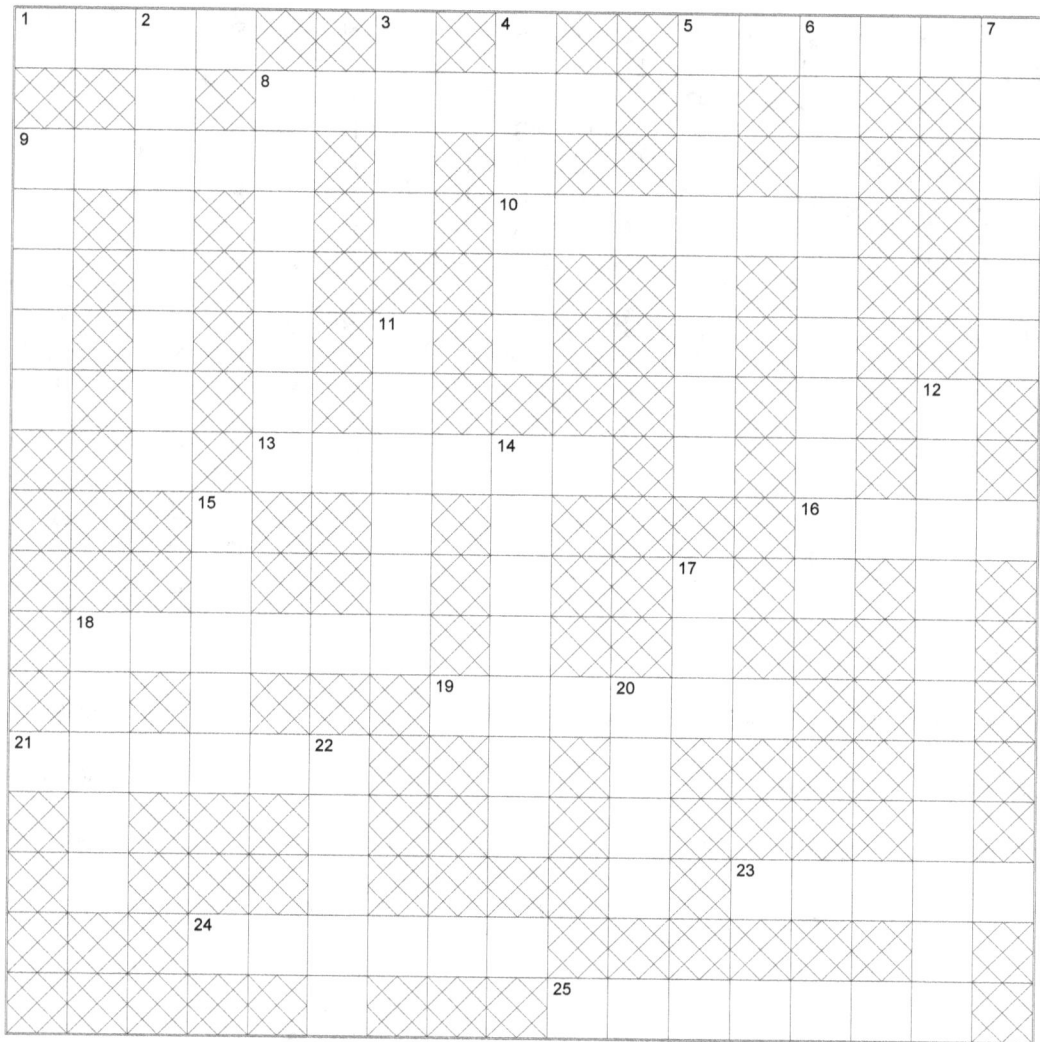

Across
1. ... not that I loved Caesar less, but that I loved ___ more
5. Servant to Brutus
8. Servant of Brutus; refused to kill Brutus
9. First to stab Caesar
10. Calpurnia tries to convince Caesar that her ____ are omens of tragedy
13. Caesar goes to this meeting
16. Soldier in army of Brutus & Cassius
18. O Julius Caesar, thou art ____ yet.
19. Devoted follower of Caesar; defeats Brutus
21. Joins and then leads the conspiracy to kill Caesar
23. Servant of Brutus
24. Wife of Brutus
25. ____, Romans, countrymen, lend me your ears.

Down
2. ____, thou art afoot, Take thou what course thou wilt.
3. Caesar, now be still. I killed not thee with half so good a ____.
4. Help, ho! They ____ Caesar!
5. Vows to follow Brutus
6. An agreement to perform together an illegal act
7. Holds Brutus's suicide sword
8. Organizes the conspiracy & gets Brutus to join
9. Antony offered Caesar one
11. Yond Cassius has a lean and ___ look.
12. Gives Caesar a letter of warning naming the conspirators
14. Liberty! Freedom! ____ is dead!
15. I have a man's mind, but a woman's ____.
17. ... that Nature might stand up/And say to all the world, 'This was a ___'
18. Beware the Ides of ___
20. Brutus thinks a just cause needs no ___ to bind the doers to their cause
22. Caesar, thou art revenged, Even with the ___ that killed thee.

Julius Caesar Crossword 1 Answer Key

	1 R	2 O	M	E		3 W		4 M		5 L	6 U	C	I	U	7 S
		I		8 C	L	I	T	U	S	I		O			T
9 C	A	S	C	A		L		R		G		N			R
		C		S		L	10 D	R	E	A	M	S			A
		H		S			E			R		P			T
		W		I		11 H	R			I		I		12 A	O
		N		E		U				U		R		A	R
			13 F	S	E	N	14 A	T	E	S		A		R	
			15 M			G	Y					16 C	A	T	O
			I			R	R		17 M			Y		E	
		18 M	I	G	H	T	Y	A		A				M	
		A		H			19 A	N	20 T	O	N	Y		I	
21 B	R	U	T	U	S	22 S		N		A				D	
		C				W		Y		T		23 V	A	R	R	O
		H			24 P	O	R	T	I	A				U	
						D				25 F	R	I	E	N	D	S

Across

1. ... not that I loved Caesar less, but that I loved ___ more
5. Servant to Brutus
8. Servant of Brutus; refused to kill Brutus
9. First to stab Caesar
10. Calpurnia tries to convince Caesar that her ____ are omens of tragedy
13. Caesar goes to this meeting
16. Soldier in army of Brutus & Cassius
18. O Julius Caesar, thou art ____ yet.
19. Devoted follower of Caesar; defeats Brutus
21. Joins and then leads the conspiracy to kill Caesar
23. Servant of Brutus
24. Wife of Brutus
25. ____, Romans, countrymen, lend me your ears.

Down

2. ____, thou art afoot, Take thou what course thou wilt.
3. Caesar, now be still. I killed not thee with half so good a ____.
4. Help, ho! They ____ Caesar!
5. Vows to follow Brutus
6. An agreement to perform together an illegal act
7. Holds Brutus's suicide sword
8. Organizes the conspiracy & gets Brutus to join
9. Antony offered Caesar one
11. Yond Cassius has a lean and ___ look.
12. Gives Caesar a letter of warning naming the conspirators
14. Liberty! Freedom! ____ is dead!
15. I have a man's mind, but a woman's ____.
17. ... that Nature might stand up/And say to all the world, 'This was a ___'
18. Beware the Ides of ___
20. Brutus thinks a just cause needs no ___ to bind the doers to their cause
22. Caesar, thou art revenged, Even with the ___ that killed thee.

Julius Caesar Crossword 2

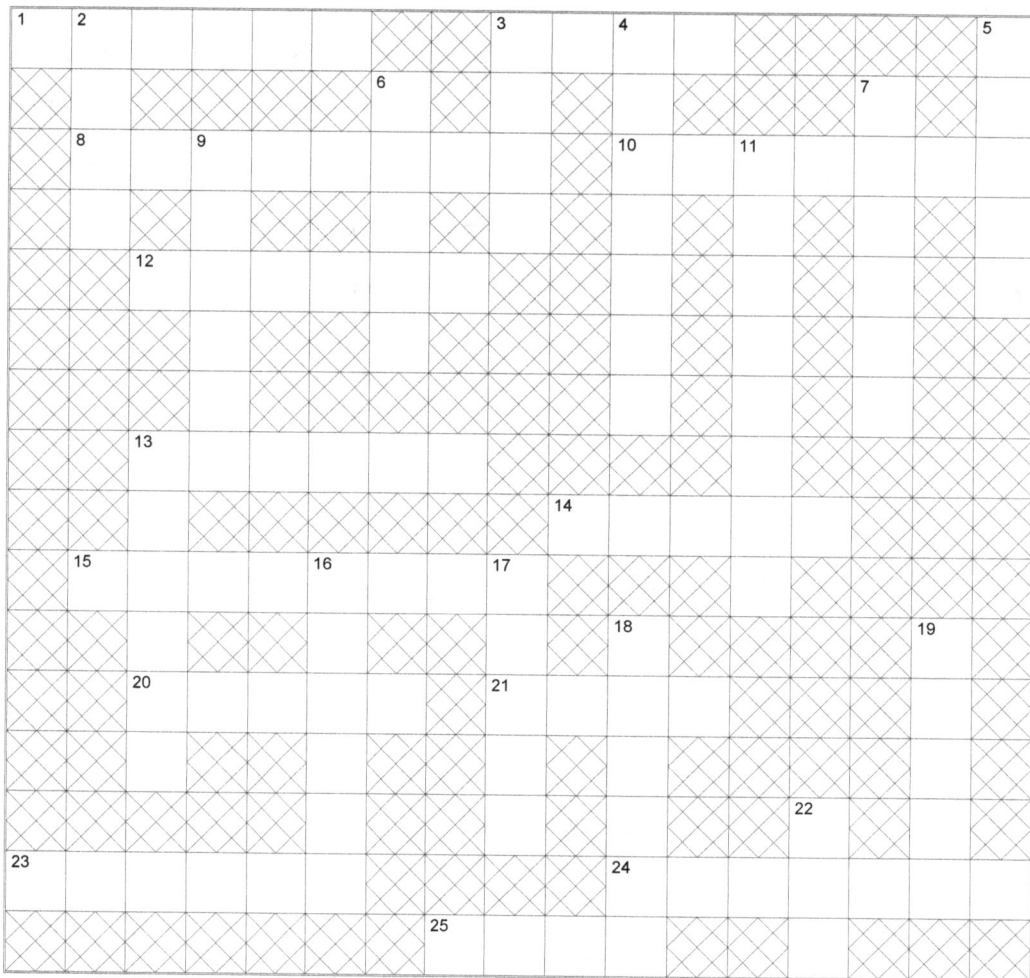

Across
1. Joins and then leads the conspiracy to kill Caesar
3. Caesar, now be still. I killed not thee with half so good a ____.
8. ____, thou art afoot, Take thou what course thou wilt.
10. One of many who escort Caesar to the Senate meeting
12. Devoted follower of Caesar; defeats Brutus
13. Reinterprets Calpurnia's dream and convinces Caesar to go to Senate
14. Servant of Brutus
15. Distracts Caesar's attention so conspirators can carry out their plan
20. Beware the Ides of ___
21. Brutus thinks a just cause needs no ___ to bind the doers to their cause
23. _____ Caesar
24. Liberty! Freedom! ____ is dead!
25. Soldier in army of Brutus & Cassius

Down
2. ... not that I loved Caesar less, but that I loved ___ more
3. Render me worthy of this noble ____!
4. Joins with Octavius and Antony and is used by them
5. First to stab Caesar
6. Plants the forged letter for Cassius
7. Roman Senator to whom Casca talks on the eve of the assassination
9. Caesar goes to this meeting
11. Let us be sacrificers, but not ____, Caius.
13. Calpurnia tries to convince Caesar that her ____ are omens of tragedy
16. Servant to Brutus
17. Caesar, thou art revenged, Even with the ___ that killed thee.
18. Holds Brutus's suicide sword
19. Antony offered Caesar one
22. ... that Nature might stand up/And say to all the world, 'This was a ___'

Julius Caesar Crossword 2 Answer Key

	1 B	2 R	U	T	U	S			3 W	4 L	L				5 C
		O					6 C		I		E			7 C	A
	8 M	9 I	S	C	H	I	E	F		10 P	U	11 B	L	I	U	S
		E		E			N		F		I		U		C	C
			12 A	N	T	O	N	Y		D		T		E	A
				A			A			U		C		R	
				T						S		H		O	
			13 D	E	C	I	U	S				E			
			R					14 V	A	R	R	O	
		15 M	E	T	E	16 L	L	17 U	S			S	
		A				U		W		18 S			19 C
		20 M	A	R	C	H		21 O	A	T	H		R
		S				I		R		R			O
						U		D		A		22 M	W
23 J	U	L	I	U	S					24 T	Y	R	A	N	N	Y
					25 C	A	T	O				N	

Across
1. Joins and then leads the conspiracy to kill Caesar
3. Caesar, now be still. I killed not thee with half so good a ____.
8. ____, thou art afoot, Take thou what course thou wilt.
10. One of many who escort Caesar to the Senate meeting
12. Devoted follower of Caesar; defeats Brutus
13. Reinterprets Calpurnia's dream and convinces Caesar to go to Senate
14. Servant of Brutus
15. Distracts Caesar's attention so conspirators can carry out their plan
20. Beware the Ides of ___
21. Brutus thinks a just cause needs no ___ to bind the doers to their cause
23. _____ Caesar
24. Liberty! Freedom! ____ is dead!
25. Soldier in army of Brutus & Cassius

Down
2. ... not that I loved Caesar less, but that I loved ___ more
3. Render me worthy of this noble ____!
4. Joins with Octavius and Antony and is used by them
5. First to stab Caesar
6. Plants the forged letter for Cassius
7. Roman Senator to whom Casca talks on the eve of the assassination
9. Caesar goes to this meeting
11. Let us be sacrificers, but not ____, Caius.
13. Calpurnia tries to convince Caesar that her ____ are omens of tragedy
16. Servant to Brutus
17. Caesar, thou art revenged, Even with the ___ that killed thee.
18. Holds Brutus's suicide sword
19. Antony offered Caesar one
22. ... that Nature might stand up/And say to all the world, 'This was a ___'

Julius Caesar Crossword 3

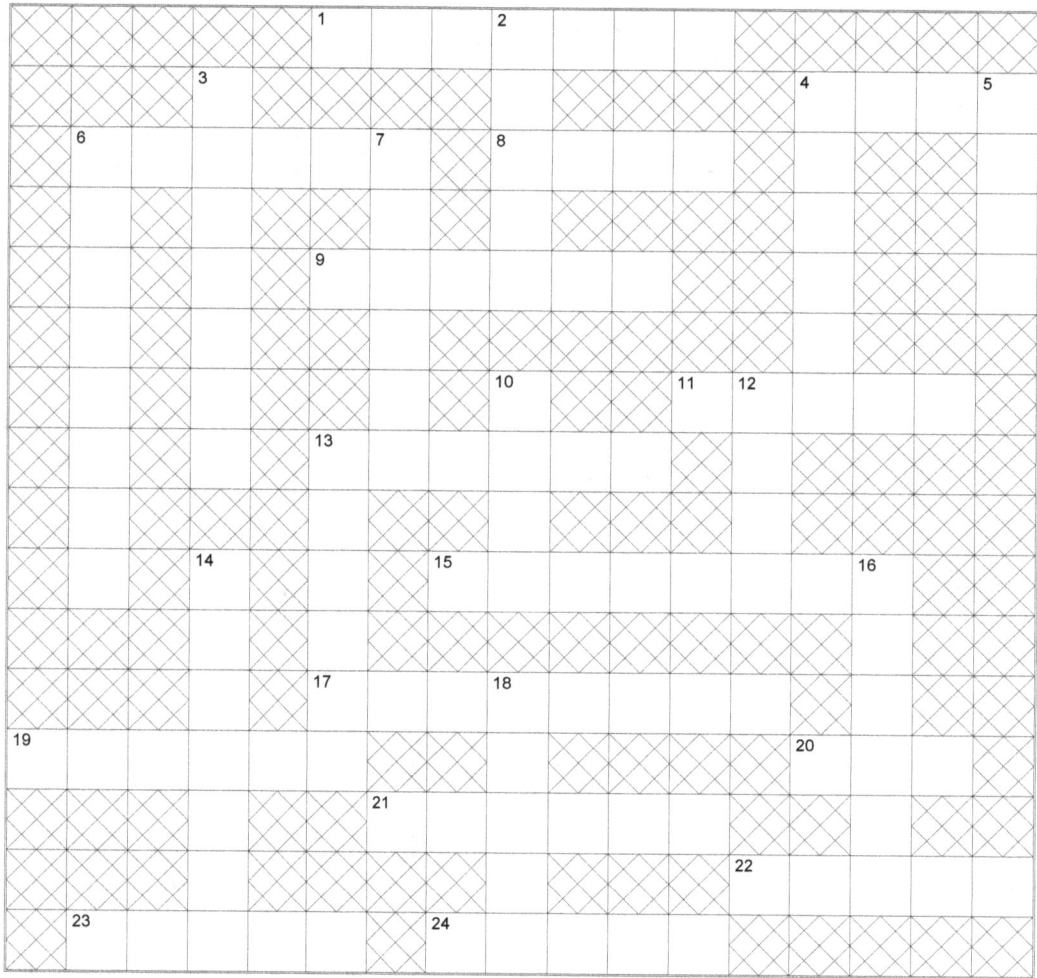

Across
1. Tribune who breaks up crowd waiting to honor Caesar's triumph
4. Soldier in army of Brutus & Cassius
6. Joins and then leads the conspiracy to kill Caesar
8. ... not that I loved Caesar less, but that I loved ___ more
9. Devoted follower of Caesar; defeats Brutus
11. Caesar, thou art revenged, Even with the ___ that killed thee.
13. Reinterprets Calpurnia's dream and convinces Caesar to go to Senate
15. Distracts Caesar's attention so conspirators can carry out their plan
17. ____, thou art afoot, Take thou what course thou wilt.
19. _____ Caesar
20. ... that Nature might stand up/And say to all the world, 'This was a ___'
21. Yond Cassius has a lean and ___ look.
22. Antony offered Caesar one
23. First to stab Caesar
24. Beware the Ides of ___

Down
2. Servant of Brutus
3. One of many who escort Caesar to the Senate meeting
4. Roman Senator to whom Casca talks on the eve of the assassination
5. Brutus thinks a just cause needs no ___ to bind the doers to their cause
6. Let us be sacrificers, but not ____, Caius.
7. Caesar goes to this meeting
10. Render me worthy of this noble ____!
12. Caesar, now be still. I killed not thee with half so good a ____.
13. Calpurnia tries to convince Caesar that her ____ are omens of tragedy
14. Joins with Octavius and Antony and is used by them
16. Holds Brutus's suicide sword
18. Plants the forged letter for Cassius

Julius Caesar Crossword 3 Answer Key

					1 F	L	A	2 V	I	U	S					
		3 P						A					4 C	A	T	5 O
6 B	R	U	T	U	7 S		8 R	O	M	E			I			A
U		B			E		R						C			T
T		L		9 A	N	T	O	N	Y				E			H
C		I		A									R			
H		U		T		10 W			11 S	W	12 O	R	D			
E		S		13 D	E	C	I	U	S		I					
R				R		F					L					
S		14 L		E		15 M	E	T	E	L	L	U	16 S			
		E		A									T			
				17 P	M	I	S	18 C	H	I	E	F		R		
19 J	U	L	I	U	S			I					20 M	A	N	
		D			21 H	U	N	G	R	Y			T			
		U						N				22 C	R	O	W	N
		23 C	A	S	C	A		24 M	A	R	C	H				

Across
1. Tribune who breaks up crowd waiting to honor Caesar's triumph
4. Soldier in army of Brutus & Cassius
6. Joins and then leads the conspiracy to kill Caesar
8. ... not that I loved Caesar less, but that I loved ___ more
9. Devoted follower of Caesar; defeats Brutus
11. Caesar, thou art revenged, Even with the ___ that killed thee.
13. Reinterprets Calpurnia's dream and convinces Caesar to go to Senate
15. Distracts Caesar's attention so conspirators can carry out their plan
17. ____, thou art afoot, Take thou what course thou wilt.
19. _____ Caesar
20. ... that Nature might stand up/And say to all the world, 'This was a ___'
21. Yond Cassius has a lean and ___ look.
22. Antony offered Caesar one
23. First to stab Caesar
24. Beware the Ides of ___

Down
2. Servant of Brutus
3. One of many who escort Caesar to the Senate meeting
4. Roman Senator to whom Casca talks on the eve of the assassination
5. Brutus thinks a just cause needs no ___ to bind the doers to their cause
6. Let us be sacrificers, but not ____, Caius.
7. Caesar goes to this meeting
10. Render me worthy of this noble ____!
12. Caesar, now be still. I killed not thee with half so good a ____.
13. Calpurnia tries to convince Caesar that her ____ are omens of tragedy
14. Joins with Octavius and Antony and is used by them
16. Holds Brutus's suicide sword
18. Plants the forged letter for Cassius

Julius Caesar Crossword 4

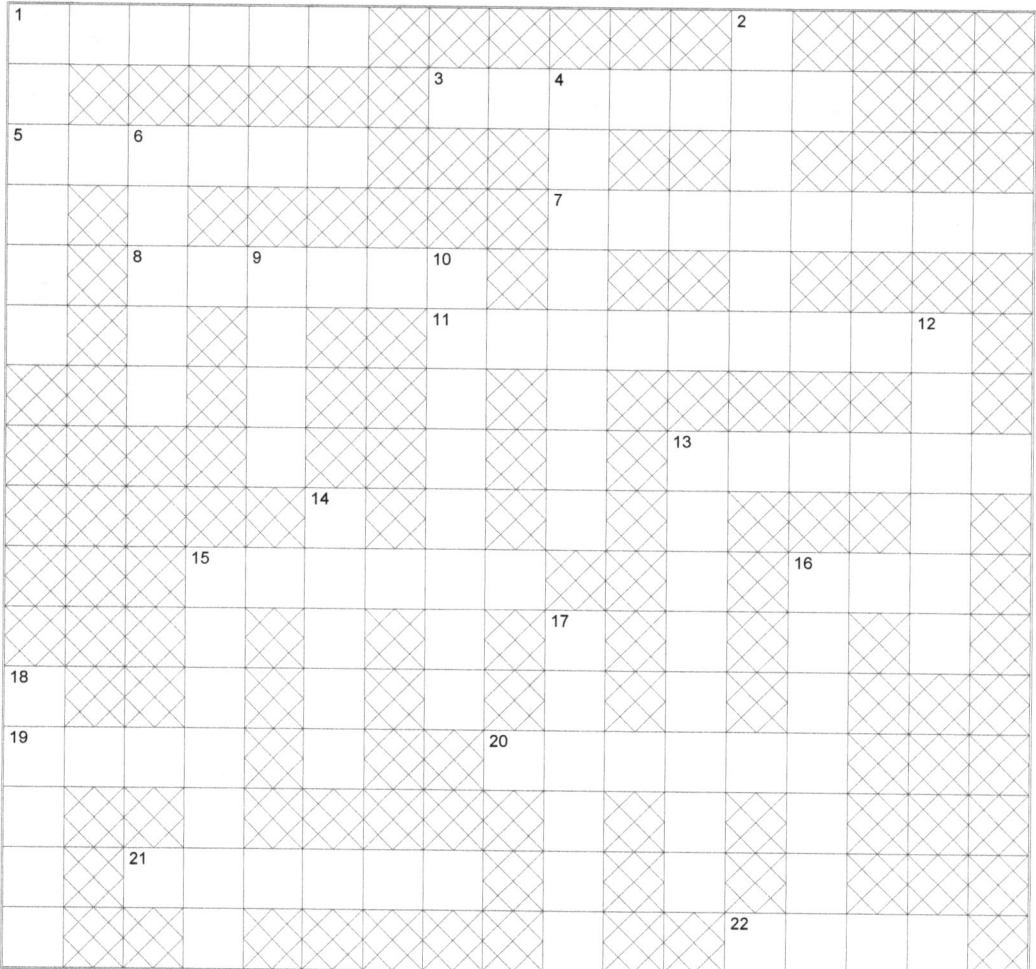

Across

1. Calpurnia tries to convince Caesar that her ____ are omens of tragedy
3. Joins with Octavius and Antony and is used by them
5. Roman Senator to whom Casca talks on the eve of the assassination
7. Servant to Cassius
8. Holds Brutus's suicide sword
11. Caesar's wife
13. O Julius Caesar, thou art ____ yet.
15. Wife of Brutus
16. ... that Nature might stand up/And say to all the world, 'This was a ___'
19. Caesar, now be still. I killed not thee with half so good a ____.
20. Servant to Brutus
21. _____ Caesar
22. Brutus thinks a just cause needs no ___ to bind the doers to their cause

Down

1. Reinterprets Calpurnia's dream and convinces Caesar to go to Senate
2. Help, ho! They ____ Caesar!
4. Wishes Cassius well in his 'enterprise'
6. First to stab Caesar
9. ... not that I loved Caesar less, but that I loved ___ more
10. Heir of Julius Caesar
12. Devoted follower of Caesar; defeats Brutus
13. ____, thou art afoot, Take thou what course thou wilt.
14. Antony offered Caesar one
15. One of many who escort Caesar to the Senate meeting
16. Reports Portia's death, discovers Cassius's body
17. Joins and then leads the conspiracy to kill Caesar
18. Caesar, thou art revenged, Even with the ___ that killed thee.

Julius Caesar Crossword 4 Answer Key

	1 D	R	E	A	M	S						2 M	
	E						3 L	E	4 P	I	D	U	S
5 C	I	6 C	E	R	O				A			R	
	I	A						7 P	I	N	D	A	R	U	S
		8 S	T	9 R	A	T	10 O		I			E	
	U												
	S	C	O			11 C	A	L	P	U	R	N	I	12 A
		A	M			T		I						N
			E			A	U		13 M	I	G	H	T	Y
					14 C		V		S		I			O
			15 P	O	R	T	I	A			S		16 M	A	N
			U		O		O		U		17 B	C	E	Y
18 S			B		W		S		R		H	S
19 W	I	L	L	N				20 L	U	C	I	U	S
O			I						T		E		A
	21 J	U	L	I	U	S			U		F		L
R	D		S						S		22 O	A	T	H

Across
1. Calpurnia tries to convince Caesar that her ____ are omens of tragedy
3. Joins with Octavius and Antony and is used by them
5. Roman Senator to whom Casca talks on the eve of the assassination
7. Servant to Cassius
8. Holds Brutus's suicide sword
11. Caesar's wife
13. O Julius Caesar, thou art ____ yet.
15. Wife of Brutus
16. ... that Nature might stand up/And say to all the world, 'This was a ___'
19. Caesar, now be still. I killed not thee with half so good a ____.
20. Servant to Brutus
21. _____ Caesar
22. Brutus thinks a just cause needs no ___ to bind the doers to their cause

Down
1. Reinterprets Calpurnia's dream and convinces Caesar to go to Senate
2. Help, ho! They ____ Caesar!
4. Wishes Cassius well in his 'enterprise'
6. First to stab Caesar
9. ... not that I loved Caesar less, but that I loved ___ more
10. Heir of Julius Caesar
12. Devoted follower of Caesar; defeats Brutus
13. ____, thou art afoot, Take thou what course thou wilt.
14. Antony offered Caesar one
15. One of many who escort Caesar to the Senate meeting
16. Reports Portia's death, discovers Cassius's body
17. Joins and then leads the conspiracy to kill Caesar
18. Caesar, thou art revenged, Even with the ___ that killed thee.

Julius Caesar

CALPURNIA	FUNERAL	MIGHT	WILL	PINDARUS
OCTAVIUS	CINNA	PAPILIUS	SWORD	LUCIUS
METELLUS	CONSPIRACY	FREE SPACE	VARRO	STRATO
WIFE	MURDER	MARCH	CLITUS	CICERO
PORTIA	VOLUMNIUS	SOOTHSAYER	LEPIDUS	CASCA

Julius Caesar

MIGHTY	CATO	FLAVIUS	TITINIUS	BRUTUS
PUBLIUS	HUNGRY	SENATE	OATH	ROME
CASSIUS	LIGARIUS	FREE SPACE	BUTCHERS	DREAMS
TYRANNY	MESSALA	ANTONY	ARTEMIDORUS	MISCHIEF
DECIUS	FRIENDS	MAN	CROWN	JULIUS

Julius Caesar

FLAVIUS	CROWN	CASCA	SENATE	STRATO
MESSALA	MIGHTY	BRUTUS	CICERO	FRIENDS
LEPIDUS	WIFE	FREE SPACE	LUCIUS	ROME
FUNERAL	PAPILIUS	VARRO	ANTONY	TREBONIUS
OATH	MARCH	MIGHT	JULIUS	PUBLIUS

Julius Caesar

METELLUS	LIGARIUS	DECIUS	MAN	TYRANNY
SWORD	CALPURNIA	CASSIUS	CLITUS	PORTIA
MURDER	TITINIUS	FREE SPACE	DREAMS	CATO
SOOTHSAYER	LUCILIUS	CINNA	CONSPIRACY	PINDARUS
MISCHIEF	WILL	BUTCHERS	VOLUMNIUS	ARTEMIDORUS

Julius Caesar

MIGHTY	DECIUS	FRIENDS	JULIUS	METELLUS
PAPILIUS	ARTEMIDORUS	WIFE	VARRO	ANTONY
CASSIUS	CALPURNIA	FREE SPACE	CINNA	STRATO
MAN	LUCILIUS	OCTAVIUS	MURDER	SENATE
BUTCHERS	PINDARUS	CATO	MESSALA	ROME

Julius Caesar

BRUTUS	TITINIUS	OATH	MARCH	TREBONIUS
PORTIA	LIGARIUS	CLITUS	MIGHT	MISCHIEF
CICERO	LEPIDUS	FREE SPACE	FUNERAL	FLAVIUS
WILL	CASCA	CONSPIRACY	HUNGRY	SOOTHSAYER
VOLUMNIUS	TYRANNY	PUBLIUS	SWORD	LUCIUS

Julius Caesar

LEPIDUS	CALPURNIA	MISCHIEF	MESSALA	STRATO
SENATE	CLITUS	WIFE	FUNERAL	ANTONY
PUBLIUS	CINNA	FREE SPACE	JULIUS	TYRANNY
BRUTUS	CASCA	TREBONIUS	CONSPIRACY	VOLUMNIUS
METELLUS	LUCILIUS	PORTIA	LIGARIUS	ARTEMIDORUS

Julius Caesar

VARRO	WILL	MARCH	CICERO	MURDER
TITINIUS	LUCIUS	MAN	CATO	SWORD
OATH	PINDARUS	FREE SPACE	DECIUS	FRIENDS
SOOTHSAYER	CROWN	ROME	OCTAVIUS	FLAVIUS
HUNGRY	BUTCHERS	MIGHTY	CASSIUS	PAPILIUS

Julius Caesar

WILL	DREAMS	CICERO	OCTAVIUS	ROME
BRUTUS	LIGARIUS	MARCH	CROWN	CASSIUS
OATH	FLAVIUS	FREE SPACE	MIGHT	JULIUS
ARTEMIDORUS	PUBLIUS	BUTCHERS	TYRANNY	LUCIUS
MESSALA	MURDER	PAPILIUS	CONSPIRACY	TREBONIUS

Julius Caesar

HUNGRY	FUNERAL	DECIUS	CALPURNIA	SENATE
METELLUS	SWORD	VARRO	FRIENDS	LUCILIUS
CINNA	CATO	FREE SPACE	MIGHTY	VOLUMNIUS
LEPIDUS	ANTONY	MAN	SOOTHSAYER	STRATO
CLITUS	PINDARUS	TITINIUS	CASCA	PORTIA

Julius Caesar

MESSALA	LIGARIUS	ROME	SENATE	METELLUS
SOOTHSAYER	ANTONY	CINNA	WILL	HUNGRY
FLAVIUS	OATH	FREE SPACE	LUCIUS	PAPILIUS
ARTEMIDORUS	TREBONIUS	PUBLIUS	BRUTUS	MIGHT
PORTIA	CASCA	CICERO	FUNERAL	CONSPIRACY

Julius Caesar

DECIUS	MIGHTY	MAN	PINDARUS	BUTCHERS
LEPIDUS	CATO	VOLUMNIUS	MURDER	FRIENDS
WIFE	VARRO	FREE SPACE	TYRANNY	LUCILIUS
SWORD	TITINIUS	MISCHIEF	STRATO	DREAMS
CROWN	MARCH	OCTAVIUS	CASSIUS	CLITUS

Julius Caesar

CATO	CICERO	CALPURNIA	LIGARIUS	CROWN
LUCIUS	PAPILIUS	VARRO	OCTAVIUS	FRIENDS
MESSALA	FLAVIUS	FREE SPACE	PUBLIUS	ARTEMIDORUS
MISCHIEF	DREAMS	MARCH	HUNGRY	CINNA
JULIUS	SENATE	PORTIA	WILL	CONSPIRACY

Julius Caesar

STRATO	MAN	ROME	SWORD	FUNERAL
WIFE	CASCA	CASSIUS	TITINIUS	DECIUS
MIGHTY	ANTONY	FREE SPACE	BUTCHERS	VOLUMNIUS
CLITUS	BRUTUS	OATH	TYRANNY	MIGHT
METELLUS	LEPIDUS	SOOTHSAYER	MURDER	PINDARUS

Julius Caesar

MURDER	JULIUS	VOLUMNIUS	MISCHIEF	METELLUS
WILL	VARRO	TYRANNY	FLAVIUS	SWORD
PAPILIUS	CALPURNIA	FREE SPACE	ROME	FRIENDS
STRATO	MIGHT	CASSIUS	CLITUS	SENATE
MESSALA	DECIUS	WIFE	PINDARUS	LUCILIUS

Julius Caesar

SOOTHSAYER	TITINIUS	OATH	OCTAVIUS	CICERO
CINNA	BUTCHERS	MARCH	CATO	CONSPIRACY
MIGHTY	ANTONY	FREE SPACE	LEPIDUS	CASCA
LUCIUS	HUNGRY	MAN	DREAMS	CROWN
FUNERAL	LIGARIUS	PORTIA	BRUTUS	PUBLIUS

Julius Caesar

WIFE	JULIUS	MARCH	MAN	CINNA
PORTIA	CONSPIRACY	CICERO	ARTEMIDORUS	FLAVIUS
CALPURNIA	FRIENDS	FREE SPACE	PINDARUS	OATH
CATO	TITINIUS	BRUTUS	CASCA	PAPILIUS
CROWN	HUNGRY	VARRO	VOLUMNIUS	SOOTHSAYER

Julius Caesar

DECIUS	CASSIUS	MIGHTY	MIGHT	MESSALA
PUBLIUS	WILL	TYRANNY	STRATO	TREBONIUS
BUTCHERS	MURDER	FREE SPACE	CLITUS	LIGARIUS
METELLUS	SENATE	LEPIDUS	ROME	OCTAVIUS
MISCHIEF	LUCILIUS	ANTONY	DREAMS	LUCIUS

Julius Caesar

MURDER	MIGHTY	LIGARIUS	FLAVIUS	PUBLIUS
CINNA	JULIUS	HUNGRY	BUTCHERS	ROME
FRIENDS	CALPURNIA	FREE SPACE	SWORD	PORTIA
CONSPIRACY	MISCHIEF	MAN	DECIUS	BRUTUS
LUCIUS	ANTONY	WIFE	SENATE	DREAMS

Julius Caesar

CATO	VOLUMNIUS	MESSALA	MARCH	CLITUS
SOOTHSAYER	ARTEMIDORUS	TREBONIUS	METELLUS	OCTAVIUS
WILL	MIGHT	FREE SPACE	STRATO	CICERO
PAPILIUS	OATH	LUCILIUS	CASSIUS	CASCA
FUNERAL	TYRANNY	PINDARUS	TITINIUS	VARRO

Julius Caesar

PUBLIUS	MURDER	LUCILIUS	CATO	MESSALA
METELLUS	FRIENDS	DECIUS	TYRANNY	OCTAVIUS
WILL	STRATO	FREE SPACE	ROME	CLITUS
CALPURNIA	CICERO	CASCA	SOOTHSAYER	MIGHT
LEPIDUS	WIFE	MIGHTY	BRUTUS	CINNA

Julius Caesar

VARRO	HUNGRY	OATH	VOLUMNIUS	MAN
FLAVIUS	PORTIA	CROWN	JULIUS	LUCIUS
TREBONIUS	BUTCHERS	FREE SPACE	CASSIUS	FUNERAL
TITINIUS	CONSPIRACY	PAPILIUS	SWORD	LIGARIUS
PINDARUS	SENATE	DREAMS	MISCHIEF	ARTEMIDORUS

Julius Caesar

MAN	STRATO	CLITUS	PAPILIUS	ANTONY
PORTIA	CALPURNIA	SWORD	JULIUS	BUTCHERS
LIGARIUS	HUNGRY	FREE SPACE	CINNA	DECIUS
MISCHIEF	ROME	CONSPIRACY	LEPIDUS	MURDER
TREBONIUS	CASCA	OCTAVIUS	SOOTHSAYER	FRIENDS

Julius Caesar

PUBLIUS	WILL	BRUTUS	FUNERAL	MIGHT
OATH	PINDARUS	MARCH	DREAMS	CATO
CICERO	LUCIUS	FREE SPACE	CASSIUS	ARTEMIDORUS
LUCILIUS	METELLUS	CROWN	VOLUMNIUS	SENATE
TYRANNY	FLAVIUS	WIFE	MESSALA	TITINIUS

Julius Caesar

VOLUMNIUS	VARRO	SWORD	MIGHT	STRATO
LIGARIUS	DECIUS	CASSIUS	MISCHIEF	FRIENDS
WILL	PINDARUS	FREE SPACE	PUBLIUS	FLAVIUS
PAPILIUS	MIGHTY	FUNERAL	JULIUS	DREAMS
METELLUS	CONSPIRACY	SOOTHSAYER	WIFE	MARCH

Julius Caesar

TYRANNY	PORTIA	LUCIUS	CICERO	CROWN
MAN	OCTAVIUS	CINNA	ANTONY	ROME
BRUTUS	TITINIUS	FREE SPACE	OATH	LEPIDUS
CATO	CALPURNIA	HUNGRY	TREBONIUS	ARTEMIDORUS
CASCA	LUCILIUS	BUTCHERS	MURDER	SENATE

Julius Caesar

CICERO	VOLUMNIUS	MESSALA	METELLUS	PORTIA
LUCIUS	SOOTHSAYER	PINDARUS	DREAMS	ARTEMIDORUS
CASCA	CONSPIRACY	FREE SPACE	MISCHIEF	TITINIUS
STRATO	CROWN	MIGHTY	LIGARIUS	SWORD
PUBLIUS	WILL	PAPILIUS	JULIUS	CINNA

Julius Caesar

DECIUS	HUNGRY	CALPURNIA	FRIENDS	MAN
SENATE	WIFE	LEPIDUS	MURDER	MARCH
FLAVIUS	TYRANNY	FREE SPACE	FUNERAL	OATH
ANTONY	BRUTUS	OCTAVIUS	CASSIUS	BUTCHERS
CATO	ROME	TREBONIUS	MIGHT	CLITUS

Julius Caesar

DREAMS	VARRO	LUCIUS	CLITUS	DECIUS
JULIUS	OCTAVIUS	HUNGRY	MARCH	ROME
BRUTUS	CASCA	FREE SPACE	STRATO	PINDARUS
MURDER	OATH	CICERO	MIGHT	SENATE
FLAVIUS	BUTCHERS	VOLUMNIUS	WIFE	METELLUS

Julius Caesar

TITINIUS	ARTEMIDORUS	LUCILIUS	LEPIDUS	MAN
FRIENDS	SOOTHSAYER	WILL	TREBONIUS	PAPILIUS
MISCHIEF	CINNA	FREE SPACE	ANTONY	CROWN
MIGHTY	CALPURNIA	SWORD	MESSALA	CASSIUS
PUBLIUS	PORTIA	CATO	FUNERAL	CONSPIRACY

Julius Caesar

MIGHT	MISCHIEF	LEPIDUS	FRIENDS	BUTCHERS
HUNGRY	LUCILIUS	PINDARUS	STRATO	MESSALA
ARTEMIDORUS	BRUTUS	FREE SPACE	PUBLIUS	LIGARIUS
MARCH	CICERO	PORTIA	CATO	WILL
CINNA	CONSPIRACY	MIGHTY	JULIUS	ANTONY

Julius Caesar

TITINIUS	VARRO	MURDER	CASCA	METELLUS
SENATE	TYRANNY	CASSIUS	WIFE	TREBONIUS
ROME	VOLUMNIUS	FREE SPACE	SOOTHSAYER	FUNERAL
DECIUS	PAPILIUS	MAN	CALPURNIA	CROWN
CLITUS	LUCIUS	DREAMS	SWORD	FLAVIUS

Julius Caesar Vocabulary Word List

No.	Word	Clue/Definition
1.	ACCOUTERED	Fully armed
2.	AFFABILITY	Friendliness; graciousness
3.	APPEASED	Soothed; pacified
4.	APPERTAIN	Belong to as a proper function or part
5.	AUGMENTED	Made greater in size, extent, or quantity
6.	AUGURERS	Professional interpreters of omens
7.	BASE	Without high values or ethics
8.	CHASTISEMENT	Punishment
9.	COFFERS	Public treasury
10.	COGITATIONS	Thoughts
11.	CONSORTED	Accompanied
12.	CONSPIRATOR	One who plans with others to commit an illegal act
13.	CONSTRUE	Interpret
14.	COVETOUS	Wanting the possessions of others
15.	EMULATION	Envy; imitation
16.	ENGENDERED	Conceived
17.	ENSIGN	Colors; flag carried
18.	ENTRAILS	Internal organs, especially intestines
19.	ENTREAT	Make an earnest request of
20.	ENVENOMED	Poisoned
21.	EXIGENT	Critical moment
22.	FAIN	Gladly
23.	INGRAFTED	Planted firmly; established
24.	LEGACIES	Inherited money or goods
25.	MALICE	Ill-will or spite
26.	MANTLE	Cloak; coat
27.	METTLE	Temperament
28.	ORATION	Formal speech
29.	PORTENTOUS	Foreboding
30.	PRODIGIES	Signs of disaster
31.	PUISSANT	Powerful; mighty
32.	STRIFE	Struggle, fight, or quarrel
33.	VISAGE	Face

Julius Caesar Vocabulary Fill In The Blanks 1

_____ 1. Wanting the possessions of others

_____ 2. Inherited money or goods

_____ 3. Struggle, fight, or quarrel

_____ 4. Critical moment

_____ 5. Interpret

_____ 6. Public treasury

_____ 7. One who plans with others to commit an illegal act

_____ 8. Foreboding

_____ 9. Ill-will or spite

_____ 10. Powerful; mighty

_____ 11. Signs of disaster

_____ 12. Make an earnest request of

_____ 13. Planted firmly; established

_____ 14. Poisoned

_____ 15. Cloak; coat

_____ 16. Accompanied

_____ 17. Face

_____ 18. Friendliness; graciousness

_____ 19. Conceived

_____ 20. Envy; imitation

Julius Caesar Vocabulary Fill In The Blanks 1 Answer Key

COVETOUS	1. Wanting the possessions of others
LEGACIES	2. Inherited money or goods
STRIFE	3. Struggle, fight, or quarrel
EXIGENT	4. Critical moment
CONSTRUE	5. Interpret
COFFERS	6. Public treasury
CONSPIRATOR	7. One who plans with others to commit an illegal act
PORTENTOUS	8. Foreboding
MALICE	9. Ill-will or spite
PUISSANT	10. Powerful; mighty
PRODIGIES	11. Signs of disaster
ENTREAT	12. Make an earnest request of
INGRAFTED	13. Planted firmly; established
ENVENOMED	14. Poisoned
MANTLE	15. Cloak; coat
CONSORTED	16. Accompanied
VISAGE	17. Face
AFFABILITY	18. Friendliness; graciousness
ENGENDERED	19. Conceived
EMULATION	20. Envy; imitation

Julius Caesar Vocabulary Fill In The Blanks 2

_____ 1. Signs of disaster

_____ 2. Cloak; coat

_____ 3. Conceived

_____ 4. Wanting the possessions of others

_____ 5. Made greater in size, extent, or quantity

_____ 6. Critical moment

_____ 7. Punishment

_____ 8. Powerful; mighty

_____ 9. Interpret

_____ 10. Soothed; pacified

_____ 11. Poisoned

_____ 12. Face

_____ 13. Friendliness; graciousness

_____ 14. Public treasury

_____ 15. Envy; imitation

_____ 16. Fully armed

_____ 17. Thoughts

_____ 18. Accompanied

_____ 19. Ill-will or spite

_____ 20. Formal speech

Julius Caesar Vocabulary Fill In The Blanks 2 Answer Key

PRODIGIES	1. Signs of disaster
MANTLE	2. Cloak; coat
ENGENDERED	3. Conceived
COVETOUS	4. Wanting the possessions of others
AUGMENTED	5. Made greater in size, extent, or quantity
EXIGENT	6. Critical moment
CHASTISEMENT	7. Punishment
PUISSANT	8. Powerful; mighty
CONSTRUE	9. Interpret
APPEASED	10. Soothed; pacified
ENVENOMED	11. Poisoned
VISAGE	12. Face
AFFABILITY	13. Friendliness; graciousness
COFFERS	14. Public treasury
EMULATION	15. Envy imitation
ACCOUTERED	16. Fully armed
COGITATIONS	17. Thoughts
CONSORTED	18. Accompanied
MALICE	19. Ill-will or spite
ORATION	20. Formal speech

Julius Caesar Vocabulary Fill In The Blanks 3

_____ 1. Powerful; mighty

_____ 2. Without high values or ethics

_____ 3. Temperament

_____ 4. Gladly

_____ 5. Internal organs, especially intestines

_____ 6. Fully armed

_____ 7. Foreboding

_____ 8. Made greater in size, extent, or quantity

_____ 9. Punishment

_____ 10. Colors; flag carried

_____ 11. Face

_____ 12. Signs of disaster

_____ 13. Interpret

_____ 14. Friendliness; graciousness

_____ 15. Thoughts

_____ 16. Wanting the possessions of others

_____ 17. Formal speech

_____ 18. Public treasury

_____ 19. Inherited money or goods

_____ 20. Critical moment

Julius Caesar Vocabulary Fill In The Blanks 3 Answer Key

PUISSANT	1.	Powerful; mighty
BASE	2.	Without high values or ethics
METTLE	3.	Temperament
FAIN	4.	Gladly
ENTRAILS	5.	Internal organs, especially intestines
ACCOUTERED	6.	Fully armed
PORTENTOUS	7.	Foreboding
AUGMENTED	8.	Made greater in size, extent, or quantity
CHASTISEMENT	9.	Punishment
ENSIGN	10.	Colors; flag carried
VISAGE	11.	Face
PRODIGIES	12.	Signs of disaster
CONSTRUE	13.	Interpret
AFFABILITY	14.	Friendliness; graciousness
COGITATIONS	15.	Thoughts
COVETOUS	16.	Wanting the possessions of others
ORATION	17.	Formal speech
COFFERS	18.	Public treasury
LEGACIES	19.	Inherited money or goods
EXIGENT	20.	Critical moment

Julius Caesar Vocabulary Fill In The Blanks 4

_____ 1. Belong to as a proper function or part

_____ 2. Struggle, fight, or quarrel

_____ 3. Powerful; mighty

_____ 4. One who plans with others to commit an illegal act

_____ 5. Inherited money or goods

_____ 6. Fully armed

_____ 7. Foreboding

_____ 8. Wanting the possessions of others

_____ 9. Professional interpreters of omens

_____ 10. Punishment

_____ 11. Without high values or ethics

_____ 12. Public treasury

_____ 13. Poisoned

_____ 14. Internal organs, especially intestines

_____ 15. Thoughts

_____ 16. Temperament

_____ 17. Signs of disaster

_____ 18. Made greater in size, extent, or quantity

_____ 19. Cloak; coat

_____ 20. Gladly

Julius Caesar Vocabulary Fill In The Blanks 4 Answer Key

APPERTAIN	1. Belong to as a proper function or part
STRIFE	2. Struggle, fight, or quarrel
PUISSANT	3. Powerful; mighty
CONSPIRATOR	4. One who plans with others to commit an illegal act
LEGACIES	5. Inherited money or goods
ACCOUTERED	6. Fully armed
PORTENTOUS	7. Foreboding
COVETOUS	8. Wanting the possessions of others
AUGURERS	9. Professional interpreters of omens
CHASTISEMENT	10. Punishment
BASE	11. Without high values or ethics
COFFERS	12. Public treasury
ENVENOMED	13. Poisoned
ENTRAILS	14. Internal organs, especially intestines
COGITATIONS	15. Thoughts
METTLE	16. Temperament
PRODIGIES	17. Signs of disaster
AUGMENTED	18. Made greater in size, extent, or quantity
MANTLE	19. Cloak; coat
FAIN	20. Gladly

Julius Caesar Vocabulary Matching 1

___ 1. PUISSANT
___ 2. STRIFE
___ 3. COFFERS
___ 4. MANTLE
___ 5. CONSPIRATOR
___ 6. CONSORTED
___ 7. APPEASED
___ 8. ENTREAT
___ 9. COGITATIONS
___ 10. PORTENTOUS
___ 11. METTLE
___ 12. AFFABILITY
___ 13. ENGENDERED
___ 14. EXIGENT
___ 15. ENVENOMED
___ 16. BASE
___ 17. AUGMENTED
___ 18. LEGACIES
___ 19. ORATION
___ 20. CHASTISEMENT
___ 21. CONSTRUE
___ 22. VISAGE
___ 23. AUGURERS
___ 24. INGRAFTED
___ 25. EMULATION

A. Punishment
B. Cloak; coat
C. One who plans with others to commit an illegal act
D. Professional interpreters of omens
E. Friendliness; graciousness
F. Critical moment
G. Soothed; pacified
H. Poisoned
I. Temperament
J. Formal speech
K. Made greater in size, extent, or quantity
L. Inherited money or goods
M. Planted firmly; established
N. Make an earnest request of
O. Envy; imitation
P. Thoughts
Q. Struggle, fight, or quarrel
R. Powerful; mighty
S. Foreboding
T. Accompanied
U. Without high values or ethics
V. Face
W. Interpret
X. Public treasury
Y. Conceived

Julius Caesar Vocabulary Matching 1 Answer Key

R - 1. PUISSANT		A. Punishment
Q - 2. STRIFE		B. Cloak; coat
X - 3. COFFERS		C. One who plans with others to commit an illegal act
B - 4. MANTLE		D. Professional interpreters of omens
C - 5. CONSPIRATOR		E. Friendliness; graciousness
T - 6. CONSORTED		F. Critical moment
G - 7. APPEASED		G. Soothed; pacified
N - 8. ENTREAT		H. Poisoned
P - 9. COGITATIONS		I. Temperament
S - 10. PORTENTOUS		J. Formal speech
I - 11. METTLE		K. Made greater in size, extent, or quantity
E - 12. AFFABILITY		L. Inherited money or goods
Y - 13. ENGENDERED		M. Planted firmly; established
F - 14. EXIGENT		N. Make an earnest request of
H - 15. ENVENOMED		O. Envy; imitation
U - 16. BASE		P. Thoughts
K - 17. AUGMENTED		Q. Struggle, fight, or quarrel
L - 18. LEGACIES		R. Powerful; mighty
J - 19. ORATION		S. Foreboding
A - 20. CHASTISEMENT		T. Accompanied
W - 21. CONSTRUE		U. Without high values or ethics
V - 22. VISAGE		V. Face
D - 23. AUGURERS		W. Interpret
M - 24. INGRAFTED		X. Public treasury
O - 25. EMULATION		Y. Conceived

Julius Caesar Vocabulary Matching 2

___ 1. COFFERS   A. Formal speech
___ 2. FAIN   B. Temperament
___ 3. CHASTISEMENT   C. Inherited money or goods
___ 4. AUGURERS   D. Face
___ 5. BASE   E. Gladly
___ 6. MANTLE   F. Public treasury
___ 7. APPEASED   G. Critical moment
___ 8. STRIFE   H. Punishment
___ 9. MALICE   I. Struggle, fight, or quarrel
___10. CONSTRUE   J. Interpret
___11. ORATION   K. Conceived
___12. AFFABILITY   L. Internal organs, especially intestines
___13. CONSORTED   M. Cloak; coat
___14. ENTREAT   N. Soothed; pacified
___15. ENGENDERED   O. Friendliness; graciousness
___16. CONSPIRATOR   P. Make an earnest request of
___17. COGITATIONS   Q. One who plans with others to commit an illegal act
___18. COVETOUS   R. Without high values or ethics
___19. AUGMENTED   S. Wanting the possessions of others
___20. APPERTAIN   T. Thoughts
___21. EXIGENT   U. Made greater in size, extent, or quantity
___22. VISAGE   V. Professional interpreters of omens
___23. ENTRAILS   W. Accompanied
___24. LEGACIES   X. Ill-will or spite
___25. METTLE   Y. Belong to as a proper function or part

Julius Caesar Vocabulary Matching 2 Answer Key

F - 1.	COFFERS	A. Formal speech
E - 2.	FAIN	B. Temperament
H - 3.	CHASTISEMENT	C. Inherited money or goods
V - 4.	AUGURERS	D. Face
R - 5.	BASE	E. Gladly
M - 6.	MANTLE	F. Public treasury
N - 7.	APPEASED	G. Critical moment
I - 8.	STRIFE	H. Punishment
X - 9.	MALICE	I. Struggle, fight, or quarrel
J - 10.	CONSTRUE	J. Interpret
A - 11.	ORATION	K. Conceived
O - 12.	AFFABILITY	L. Internal organs, especially intestines
W - 13.	CONSORTED	M. Cloak; coat
P - 14.	ENTREAT	N. Soothed; pacified
K - 15.	ENGENDERED	O. Friendliness; graciousness
Q - 16.	CONSPIRATOR	P. Make an earnest request of
T - 17.	COGITATIONS	Q. One who plans with others to commit an illegal act
S - 18.	COVETOUS	R. Without high values or ethics
U - 19.	AUGMENTED	S. Wanting the possessions of others
Y - 20.	APPERTAIN	T. Thoughts
G - 21.	EXIGENT	U. Made greater in size, extent, or quantity
D - 22.	VISAGE	V. Professional interpreters of omens
L - 23.	ENTRAILS	W. Accompanied
C - 24.	LEGACIES	X. Ill-will or spite
B - 25.	METTLE	Y. Belong to as a proper function or part

Julius Caesar Vocabulary Matching 3

___ 1. MALICE
___ 2. ORATION
___ 3. STRIFE
___ 4. ENTREAT
___ 5. COFFERS
___ 6. VISAGE
___ 7. PUISSANT
___ 8. APPERTAIN
___ 9. APPEASED
___ 10. FAIN
___ 11. ENSIGN
___ 12. ENTRAILS
___ 13. LEGACIES
___ 14. PRODIGIES
___ 15. AUGMENTED
___ 16. AFFABILITY
___ 17. AUGURERS
___ 18. CONSPIRATOR
___ 19. ACCOUTERED
___ 20. INGRAFTED
___ 21. PORTENTOUS
___ 22. METTLE
___ 23. ENVENOMED
___ 24. ENGENDERED
___ 25. COGITATIONS

A. Thoughts
B. Ill-will or spite
C. Inherited money or goods
D. Poisoned
E. Fully armed
F. Gladly
G. Face
H. Temperament
I. Struggle, fight, or quarrel
J. Colors; flag carried
K. One who plans with others to commit an illegal act
L. Foreboding
M. Formal speech
N. Make an earnest request of
O. Planted firmly; established
P. Powerful; mighty
Q. Soothed; pacified
R. Public treasury
S. Friendliness; graciousness
T. Conceived
U. Signs of disaster
V. Made greater in size, extent, or quantity
W. Professional interpreters of omens
X. Internal organs, especially intestines
Y. Belong to as a proper function or part

Julius Caesar Vocabulary Matching 3 Answer Key

B - 1. MALICE		A. Thoughts
M - 2. ORATION		B. Ill-will or spite
I - 3. STRIFE		C. Inherited money or goods
N - 4. ENTREAT		D. Poisoned
R - 5. COFFERS		E. Fully armed
G - 6. VISAGE		F. Gladly
P - 7. PUISSANT		G. Face
Y - 8. APPERTAIN		H. Temperament
Q - 9. APPEASED		I. Struggle, fight, or quarrel
F - 10. FAIN		J. Colors; flag carried
J - 11. ENSIGN		K. One who plans with others to commit an illegal act
X - 12. ENTRAILS		L. Foreboding
C - 13. LEGACIES		M. Formal speech
U - 14. PRODIGIES		N. Make an earnest request of
V - 15. AUGMENTED		O. Planted firmly; established
S - 16. AFFABILITY		P. Powerful; mighty
W - 17. AUGURERS		Q. Soothed; pacified
K - 18. CONSPIRATOR		R. Public treasury
E - 19. ACCOUTERED		S. Friendliness; graciousness
O - 20. INGRAFTED		T. Conceived
L - 21. PORTENTOUS		U. Signs of disaster
H - 22. METTLE		V. Made greater in size, extent, or quantity
D - 23. ENVENOMED		W. Professional interpreters of omens
T - 24. ENGENDERED		X. Internal organs, especially intestines
A - 25. COGITATIONS		Y. Belong to as a proper function or part

Julius Caesar Vocabulary Matching 4

___ 1. EXIGENT			A. Colors; flag carried
___ 2. AFFABILITY		B. Accompanied
___ 3. AUGMENTED		C. Internal organs, especially intestines
___ 4. PUISSANT			D. Powerful; mighty
___ 5. ENTREAT			E. Envy; imitation
___ 6. STRIFE			F. Planted firmly; established
___ 7. APPEASED			G. Belong to as a proper function or part
___ 8. EMULATION		H. Struggle, fight, or quarrel
___ 9. PORTENTOUS		I. Friendliness; graciousness
___ 10. CONSORTED		J. Signs of disaster
___ 11. ACCOUTERED		K. Cloak; coat
___ 12. CONSTRUE		L. Interpret
___ 13. ENVENOMED		M. Make an earnest request of
___ 14. LEGACIES		N. Poisoned
___ 15. ENSIGN			O. Fully armed
___ 16. APPERTAIN		P. Formal speech
___ 17. VISAGE			Q. Soothed; pacified
___ 18. PRODIGIES		R. Without high values or ethics
___ 19. ENTRAILS		S. Critical moment
___ 20. CONSPIRATOR		T. Inherited money or goods
___ 21. INGRAFTED		U. Conceived
___ 22. ENGENDERED		V. Made greater in size, extent, or quantity
___ 23. ORATION			W. One who plans with others to commit an illegal act
___ 24. BASE			X. Face
___ 25. MANTLE			Y. Foreboding

Julius Caesar Vocabulary Matching 4 Answer Key

S - 1. EXIGENT — A. Colors; flag carried
I - 2. AFFABILITY — B. Accompanied
V - 3. AUGMENTED — C. Internal organs, especially intestines
D - 4. PUISSANT — D. Powerful; mighty
M - 5. ENTREAT — E. Envy; imitation
H - 6. STRIFE — F. Planted firmly; established
Q - 7. APPEASED — G. Belong to as a proper function or part
E - 8. EMULATION — H. Struggle, fight, or quarrel
Y - 9. PORTENTOUS — I. Friendliness; graciousness
B - 10. CONSORTED — J. Signs of disaster
O - 11. ACCOUTERED — K. Cloak; coat
L - 12. CONSTRUE — L. Interpret
N - 13. ENVENOMED — M. Make an earnest request of
T - 14. LEGACIES — N. Poisoned
A - 15. ENSIGN — O. Fully armed
G - 16. APPERTAIN — P. Formal speech
X - 17. VISAGE — Q. Soothed; pacified
J - 18. PRODIGIES — R. Without high values or ethics
C - 19. ENTRAILS — S. Critical moment
W - 20. CONSPIRATOR — T. Inherited money or goods
F - 21. INGRAFTED — U. Conceived
U - 22. ENGENDERED — V. Made greater in size, extent, or quantity
P - 23. ORATION — W. One who plans with others to commit an illegal act
R - 24. BASE — X. Face
K - 25. MANTLE — Y. Foreboding

Julius Caesar Vocabulary Magic Squares 1

Match the definition with the vocabulary word. Put your answers in the magic squares below. When your answers are correct, all columns and rows will add to the same number.

A. COFFERS
B. ACCOUTERED
C. PRODIGIES
D. AUGURERS
E. EMULATION
F. INGRAFTED
G. EXIGENT
H. ENGENDERED
I. CONSTRUE
J. ENVENOMED
K. METTLE
L. FAIN
M. LEGACIES
N. AFFABILITY
O. ORATION
P. PUISSANT

1. Fully armed
2. Critical moment
3. Temperament
4. Friendliness; graciousness
5. Inherited money or goods
6. Gladly
7. Conceived
8. Public treasury
9. Powerful; mighty
10. Interpret
11. Envy; imitation
12. Professional interpreters of omens
13. Signs of disaster
14. Planted firmly; established
15. Poisoned
16. Formal speech

A=	B=	C=	D=
E=	F=	G=	H=
I=	J=	K=	L=
M=	N=	O=	P=

79
Copyrighted

Julius Caesar Vocabulary Magic Squares 1 Answer Key

Match the definition with the vocabulary word. Put your answers in the magic squares below. When your answers are correct, all columns and rows will add to the same number.

A. COFFERS
B. ACCOUTERED
C. PRODIGIES
D. AUGURERS
E. EMULATION
F. INGRAFTED
G. EXIGENT
H. ENGENDERED
I. CONSTRUE
J. ENVENOMED
K. METTLE
L. FAIN
M. LEGACIES
N. AFFABILITY
O. ORATION
P. PUISSANT

1. Fully armed
2. Critical moment
3. Temperament
4. Friendliness; graciousness
5. Inherited money or goods
6. Gladly
7. Conceived
8. Public treasury
9. Powerful; mighty
10. Interpret
11. Envy; imitation
12. Professional interpreters of omens
13. Signs of disaster
14. Planted firmly; established
15. Poisoned
16. Formal speech

A=8	B=1	C=13	D=12
E=11	F=14	G=2	H=7
I=10	J=15	K=3	L=6
M=5	N=4	O=16	P=9

Julius Caesar Vocabulary Magic Squares 2

Match the definition with the vocabulary word. Put your answers in the magic squares below. When your answers are correct, all columns and rows will add to the same number.

A. COGITATIONS
B. ENSIGN
C. VISAGE
D. INGRAFTED
E. ENGENDERED
F. METTLE
G. LEGACIES
H. ACCOUTERED
I. ORATION
J. CONSTRUE
K. PUISSANT
L. MANTLE
M. CONSORTED
N. COFFERS
O. APPERTAIN
P. ENTREAT

1. Face
2. Interpret
3. Temperament
4. Belong to as a proper function or part
5. Make an earnest request of
6. Conceived
7. Formal speech
8. Planted firmly; established
9. Accompanied
10. Fully armed
11. Cloak; coat
12. Thoughts
13. Colors; flag carried
14. Powerful; mighty
15. Inherited money or goods
16. Public treasury

A=	B=	C=	D=
E=	F=	G=	H=
I=	J=	K=	L=
M=	N=	O=	P=

Julius Caesar Vocabulary Magic Squares 2 Answer Key

Match the definition with the vocabulary word. Put your answers in the magic squares below. When your answers are correct, all columns and rows will add to the same number.

A. COGITATIONS
B. ENSIGN
C. VISAGE
D. INGRAFTED
E. ENGENDERED
F. METTLE
G. LEGACIES
H. ACCOUTERED
I. ORATION
J. CONSTRUE
K. PUISSANT
L. MANTLE
M. CONSORTED
N. COFFERS
O. APPERTAIN
P. ENTREAT

1. Face
2. Interpret
3. Temperament
4. Belong to as a proper function or part
5. Make an earnest request of
6. Conceived
7. Formal speech
8. Planted firmly; established
9. Accompanied
10. Fully armed
11. Cloak; coat
12. Thoughts
13. Colors; flag carried
14. Powerful; mighty
15. Inherited money or goods
16. Public treasury

A=12	B=13	C=1	D=8
E=6	F=3	G=15	H=10
I=7	J=2	K=14	L=11
M=9	N=16	O=4	P=5

Julius Caesar Vocabulary Magic Squares 3

Match the definition with the vocabulary word. Put your answers in the magic squares below. When your answers are correct, all columns and rows will add to the same number.

A. EXIGENT
B. PORTENTOUS
C. INGRAFTED
D. AUGURERS
E. COGITATIONS
F. AUGMENTED
G. ENVENOMED
H. COVETOUS
I. APPEASED
J. METTLE
K. EMULATION
L. PUISSANT
M. AFFABILITY
N. BASE
O. ACCOUTERED
P. LEGACIES

1. Wanting the possessions of others
2. Critical moment
3. Foreboding
4. Poisoned
5. Temperament
6. Fully armed
7. Inherited money or goods
8. Soothed; pacified
9. Envy; imitation
10. Without high values or ethics
11. Friendliness; graciousness
12. Powerful; mighty
13. Thoughts
14. Professional interpreters of omens
15. Planted firmly; established
16. Made greater in size, extent, or quantity

A=	B=	C=	D=
E=	F=	G=	H=
I=	J=	K=	L=
M=	N=	O=	P=

83
Copyrighted

Julius Caesar Vocabulary Magic Squares 3 Answer Key

Match the definition with the vocabulary word. Put your answers in the magic squares below. When your answers are correct, all columns and rows will add to the same number.

A. EXIGENT
B. PORTENTOUS
C. INGRAFTED
D. AUGURERS
E. COGITATIONS
F. AUGMENTED
G. ENVENOMED
H. COVETOUS
I. APPEASED
J. METTLE
K. EMULATION
L. PUISSANT
M. AFFABILITY
N. BASE
O. ACCOUTERED
P. LEGACIES

1. Wanting the possessions of others
2. Critical moment
3. Foreboding
4. Poisoned
5. Temperament
6. Fully armed
7. Inherited money or goods
8. Soothed; pacified
9. Envy; imitation
10. Without high values or ethics
11. Friendliness; graciousness
12. Powerful; mighty
13. Thoughts
14. Professional interpreters of omens
15. Planted firmly; established
16. Made greater in size, extent, or quantity

A=2	B=3	C=15	D=14
E=13	F=16	G=4	H=1
I=8	J=5	K=9	L=12
M=11	N=10	O=6	P=7

Julius Caesar Vocabulary Magic Squares 4

Match the definition with the vocabulary word. Put your answers in the magic squares below. When your answers are correct, all columns and rows will add to the same number.

A. ENSIGN
B. BASE
C. METTLE
D. MALICE
E. ENTREAT
F. APPEASED
G. LEGACIES
H. ENVENOMED
I. PUISSANT
J. AUGMENTED
K. COFFERS
L. INGRAFTED
M. APPERTAIN
N. COVETOUS
O. CHASTISEMENT
P. STRIFE

1. Colors; flag carried
2. Wanting the possessions of others
3. Made greater in size, extent, or quantity
4. Make an earnest request of
5. Inherited money or goods
6. Planted firmly; established
7. Struggle, fight, or quarrel
8. Temperament
9. Punishment
10. Ill-will or spite
11. Poisoned
12. Public treasury
13. Powerful; mighty
14. Soothed; pacified
15. Without high values or ethics
16. Belong to as a proper function or part

A=	B=	C=	D=
E=	F=	G=	H=
I=	J=	K=	L=
M=	N=	O=	P=

Julius Caesar Vocabulary Magic Squares 4 Answer Key

Match the definition with the vocabulary word. Put your answers in the magic squares below. When your answers are correct, all columns and rows will add to the same number.

A. ENSIGN
B. BASE
C. METTLE
D. MALICE
E. ENTREAT
F. APPEASED
G. LEGACIES
H. ENVENOMED
I. PUISSANT
J. AUGMENTED
K. COFFERS
L. INGRAFTED
M. APPERTAIN
N. COVETOUS
O. CHASTISEMENT
P. STRIFE

1. Colors; flag carried
2. Wanting the possessions of others
3. Made greater in size, extent, or quantity
4. Make an earnest request of
5. Inherited money or goods
6. Planted firmly; established
7. Struggle, fight, or quarrel
8. Temperament
9. Punishment
10. Ill-will or spite
11. Poisoned
12. Public treasury
13. Powerful; mighty
14. Soothed; pacified
15. Without high values or ethics
16. Belong to as a proper function or part

A=1	B=15	C=8	D=10
E=4	F=14	G=5	H=11
I=13	J=3	K=12	L=6
M=16	N=2	O=9	P=7

Julius Caesar Vocabulary Word Search 1

Words are placed backwards, forward, diagonally, up and down. Clues listed below can help you find the words. Circle the hidden vocabulary words in the maze.

```
F K J H N T C K V N G N F G J X N S D S G
K Y P C D M N G D T K X C M W A H B C Q R
C J S U O T N E T R O P D H P G V O D X N
O K T G C Z M N R J H H Y P J L N D Y K M
N M R L W O D E Q P M F E D M S N P M N N
S T C D N F N N G N M R K D P G M N A A H
T C X E D R P S F H T G B I S B Y K L U X
R R V X S X F I O A K N R Q E W W L I G B
U N V P K A E G I R O A G T I N W E C M W
E G A S I V S N O I T A T I G O C N E E P
K N V N S R X D T O M E J A I I H G S N K
W J T G L W P A R R B L D P D T A E A T W
L K N R H H L X L A A V Z P E R S N B E H
P L A Y E U C D Y C S I T A P O I E D C C
S C S S M A B W Y S C D L S Y J S R V A R
X P S E F Z T W C O K D D S E B L E E F G
W W I D C S A M T U E G S E D J S M D F B
Z F U F S E U M E T T L E D J R P E V O A P
N P P F J I G F F E M M T J E M L N X B Z
K T M T T C U A I R X W J B M G T W U I F
M P A V J A R Q R E X I F Q W T H S L H
P V N P G G E Y T D S F G E Y J F S D T P
L T T H N E R G S M O T L T N B Q M N Y F
C G L I R L S B J C R M F B Q T M G P C R
D B E B R W X H C P W B R K C T M G P C R
```

Accompanied (9)
Belong to as a proper function or part (9)
Cloak; coat (6)
Colors; flag carried (6)
Conceived (10)
Critical moment (7)
Envy; imitation (9)
Face (6)
Foreboding (10)
Formal speech (7)
Friendliness; graciousness (10)
Fully armed (10)
Gladly (4)
Ill-will or spite (6)
Inherited money or goods (8)
Internal organs, especially intestines (8)
Interpret (8)
Made greater in size, extent, or quantity (9)
Make an earnest request of (7)
One who plans with others to commit an illegal act (11)

Planted firmly; established (9)
Poisoned (9)
Powerful; mighty (8)
Professional interpreters of omens (8)
Public treasury (7)
Punishment (12)
Signs of disaster (9)
Soothed; pacified (8)
Struggle, fight, or quarrel (6)
Temperament (6)
Thoughts (11)
Wanting the possessions of others (8)
Without high values or ethics (4)

Julius Caesar Vocabulary Word Search 1 Answer Key

Words are placed backwards, forward, diagonally, up and down. Clues listed below can help you find the words. Circle the hidden vocabulary words in the maze.

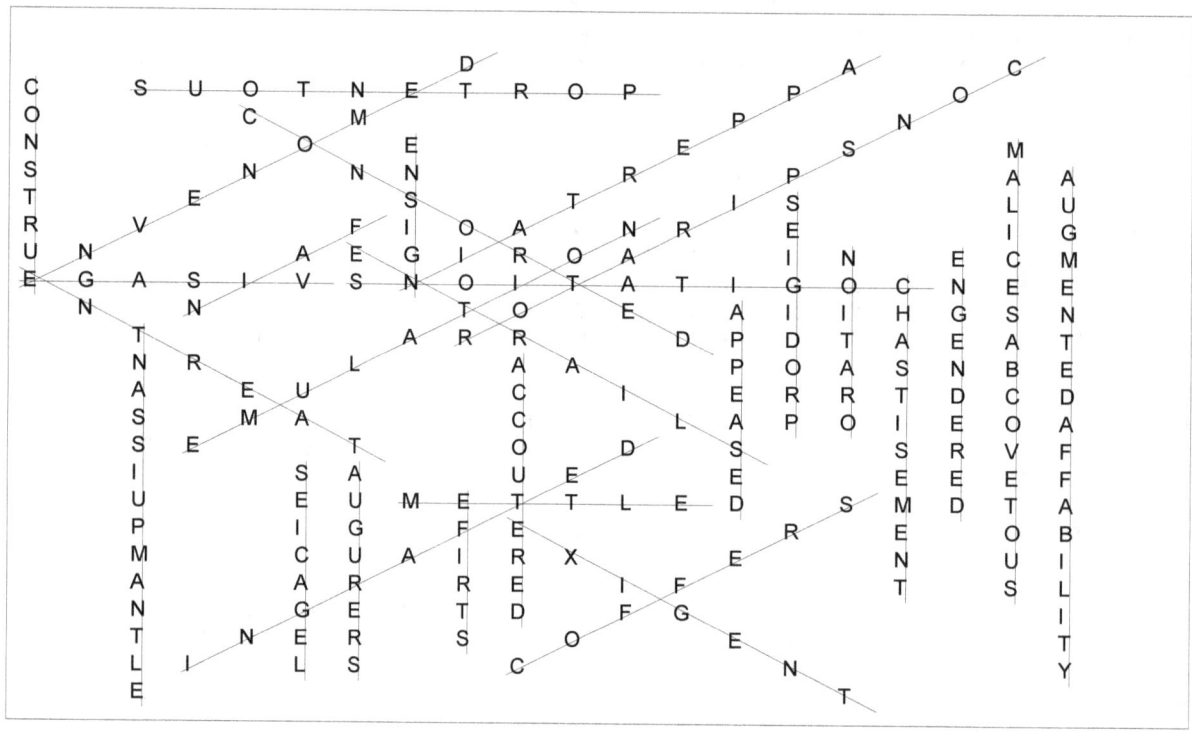

Accompanied (9)
Belong to as a proper function or part (9)
Cloak; coat (6)
Colors; flag carried (6)
Conceived (10)
Critical moment (7)
Envy; imitation (9)
Face (6)
Foreboding (10)
Formal speech (7)
Friendliness; graciousness (10)
Fully armed (10)
Gladly (4)
Ill-will or spite (6)
Inherited money or goods (8)
Internal organs, especially intestines (8)
Interpret (8)
Made greater in size, extent, or quantity (9)
Make an earnest request of (7)
One who plans with others to commit an illegal act (11)

Planted firmly; established (9)
Poisoned (9)
Powerful; mighty (8)
Professional interpreters of omens (8)
Public treasury (7)
Punishment (12)
Signs of disaster (9)
Soothed; pacified (8)
Struggle, fight, or quarrel (6)
Temperament (6)
Thoughts (11)
Wanting the possessions of others (8)
Without high values or ethics (4)

Julius Caesar Vocabulary Word Search 2

Words are placed backwards, forward, diagonally, up and down. Clues listed below can help you find the words. Circle the hidden vocabulary words in the maze.

```
P R C P C O V E T O U S A P P E R T A I N
R C O W U Z L H T V M L F W E B V N X C X
O P N T L I Z Y R Q A Q F T N P Q E H V Y
D S S D T H S M R L C F A V V N V M Q Q R
I Q P S J R X S B W C P B F E Y R E T V S
G S I T T B V Y A G O R I J N H P S Q P J
I Y R H B T S Z S N U D L C O C L I N P P
E T A Q N B Z D B X T Q I R M H V T K L C
S J T J H T N D S H E F T V E W Y S P Z C
N Q O K C R V Z N G R G Y Q D K E A N C C
W C R G K Q Q V O S E T Z H L G M H K A N
W Q J T X S M B I V D G A H F V U C V P D
S T T C V L L P T N C F U R X L L N V P H
U E F N C I T M A F C S G N H C A Z S E R
O T N K Z A D D T E W H U W R I T E Q A Y
T C Y G F R J X I B N Y R S N K I U T S C
N T B W E T J S G S C T E G Y M O R M E Z
E X I G E N T C O N S O R T E D N T O D P
T F N K G E D P C C C A S E P M M S R P S
R A P I G L S E O B F Y L F A G B N A P E
O I S A R T N F R T X L Z Z W T N O T C M
P N S R T F P E E S A B L E G A C I E S S
E I V I M E Q D W K D X Z P S S M L O F M
V H F S R M G T L S N S B C K D A P N B J
Z E C S A U G M E N T E D W Y M A N T L E
```

Accompanied (9)
Belong to as a proper function or part (9)
Cloak; coat (6)
Colors; flag carried (6)
Conceived (10)
Critical moment (7)
Envy; imitation (9)
Face (6)
Foreboding (10)
Formal speech (7)
Friendliness; graciousness (10)
Fully armed (10)
Gladly (4)
Ill-will or spite (6)
Inherited money or goods (8)
Internal organs, especially intestines (8)
Interpret (8)
Made greater in size, extent, or quantity (9)
Make an earnest request of (7)
One who plans with others to commit an illegal act (11)

Planted firmly; established (9)
Poisoned (9)
Powerful; mighty (8)
Professional interpreters of omens (8)
Public treasury (7)
Punishment (12)
Signs of disaster (9)
Soothed; pacified (8)
Struggle, fight, or quarrel (6)
Temperament (6)
Thoughts (11)
Wanting the possessions of others (8)
Without high values or ethics (4)

Julius Caesar Vocabulary Word Search 2 Answer Key

Words are placed backwards, forward, diagonally, up and down. Clues listed below can help you find the words. Circle the hidden vocabulary words in the maze.

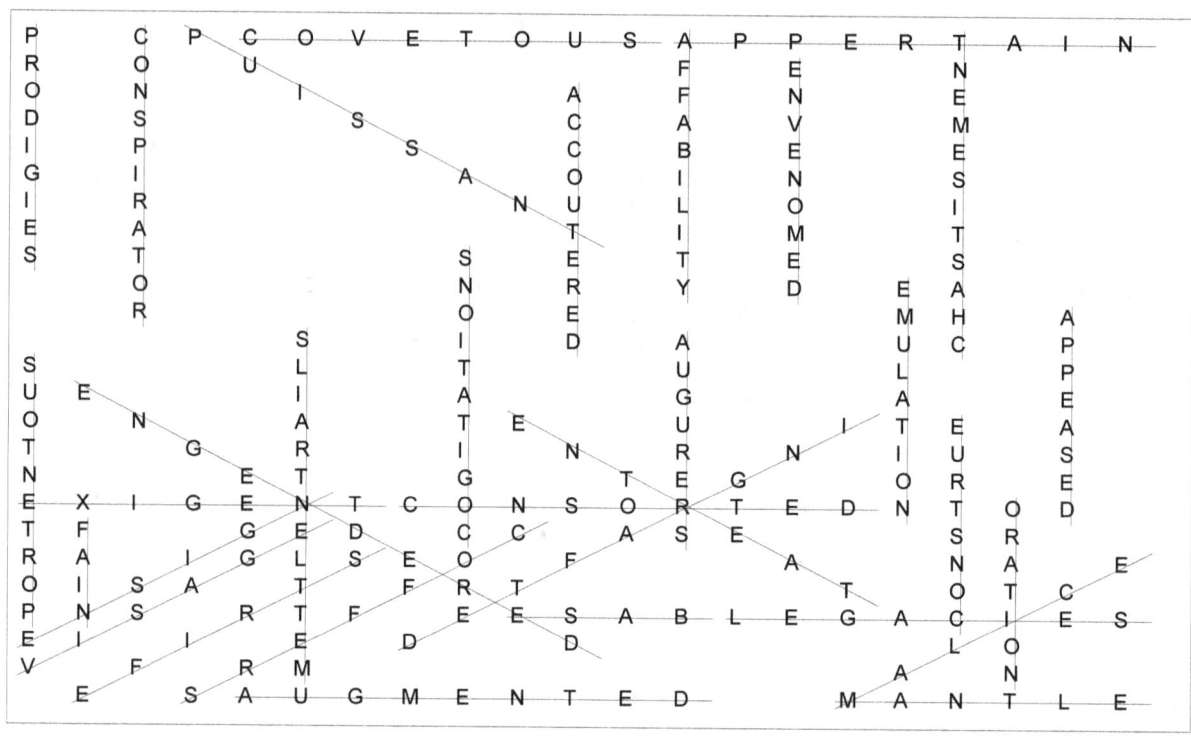

Accompanied (9)
Belong to as a proper function or part (9)
Cloak; coat (6)
Colors; flag carried (6)
Conceived (10)
Critical moment (7)
Envy; imitation (9)
Face (6)
Foreboding (10)
Formal speech (7)
Friendliness; graciousness (10)
Fully armed (10)
Gladly (4)
Ill-will or spite (6)
Inherited money or goods (8)
Internal organs, especially intestines (8)
Interpret (8)
Made greater in size, extent, or quantity (9)
Make an earnest request of (7)
One who plans with others to commit an
  illegal act (11)

Planted firmly; established (9)
Poisoned (9)
Powerful; mighty (8)
Professional interpreters of omens (8)
Public treasury (7)
Punishment (12)
Signs of disaster (9)
Soothed; pacified (8)
Struggle, fight, or quarrel (6)
Temperament (6)
Thoughts (11)
Wanting the possessions of others (8)
Without high values or ethics (4)

Julius Caesar Vocabulary Word Search 3

Words are placed backwards, forward, diagonally, up and down. Words listed below are included in the maze. Circle the hidden vocabulary words in the maze.

```
F N K C O N S P I R A T O R H Q C H F A Y
H Q C C B T J J N B X K K C T M O Z L P B
J K K K F S C P Z H J J K T W C G F B P D
J R H A C H A S T I S E M E N T I D B E W
M E J S U W K T S Q K V W B K G T E G R G
Y L N L F G T S U N T K Q R H R A M L T Q
B Q N G V B M B O D G S D K A S T O V A M
L N Z K E F H E T J Y E Y G P J I N M I C
B Q R R C N V J N P M I Y J P H O E N N Y
P Q P Q W F D C E T T G V Y E X N V F H S
J Y V B P E O E T Q E I M G A E S N D R X
P Z N C O N S O R T E D V I S A G E E P B
X C X H S S F Z O E E O J A E B R F X U Y
J D S T D I S S P T D R B L D E F K I I P
W R R G W G G F F S G P P R T O O T G S V
T U F A I N G A E P Y B N U C E R M E S R
E N C S C J R L N F X O O Q C N A Y N A D
F B O S R G T R T F I C X I S T T L T N M
V J V Y N T D B R T C P L R B R I Z B T H
N T E I E F J S A A K A E R F E O R F E L
D Z T M F F T L I Q M R N S K A N D L F C
K Q O Q H G U K L L U C L N Y T T T H I G
R K U G D M T S S G F L G Y Z B N H J R T
V F S N E J D P U X P S E I C A G E L T P
S Y T I L I B A F F A G L N M L S M X S D
```

ACCOUTERED	COGITATIONS	ENTREAT	ORATION
AFFABILITY	CONSORTED	ENVENOMED	PORTENTOUS
APPEASED	CONSPIRATOR	EXIGENT	PRODIGIES
APPERTAIN	CONSTRUE	FAIN	PUISSANT
AUGMENTED	COVETOUS	INGRAFTED	STRIFE
AUGURERS	EMULATION	LEGACIES	VISAGE
BASE	ENGENDERED	MALICE	
CHASTISEMENT	ENSIGN	MANTLE	
COFFERS	ENTRAILS	METTLE	

Julius Caesar Vocabulary Word Search 3 Answer Key

Words are placed backwards, forward, diagonally, up and down. Words listed below are included in the maze. Circle the hidden vocabulary words in the maze.

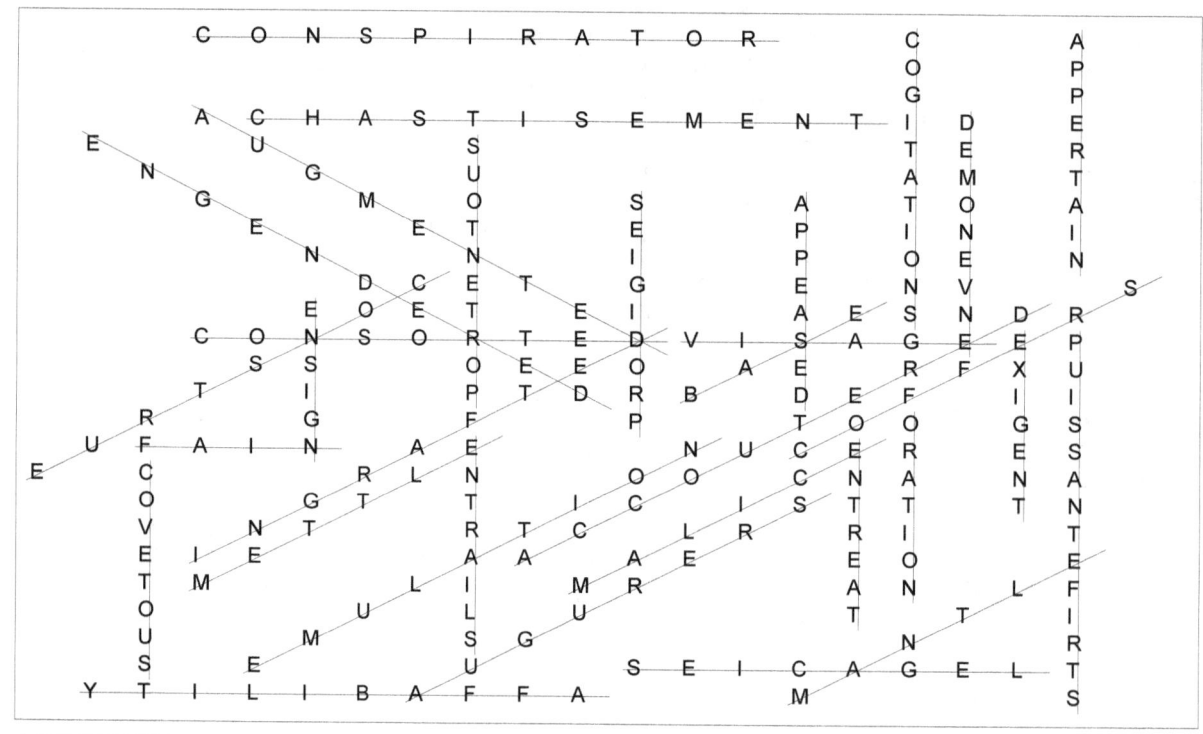

ACCOUTERED	COGITATIONS	ENTREAT	ORATION
AFFABILITY	CONSORTED	ENVENOMED	PORTENTOUS
APPEASED	CONSPIRATOR	EXIGENT	PRODIGIES
APPERTAIN	CONSTRUE	FAIN	PUISSANT
AUGMENTED	COVETOUS	INGRAFTED	STRIFE
AUGURERS	EMULATION	LEGACIES	VISAGE
BASE	ENGENDERED	MALICE	
CHASTISEMENT	ENSIGN	MANTLE	
COFFERS	ENTRAILS	METTLE	

Julius Caesar Vocabulary Word Search 4

Words are placed backwards, forward, diagonally, up and down. Words listed below are included in the maze. Circle the hidden vocabulary words in the maze.

```
Z C S A Q X P A F F A B I L I T Y L I D X
M O V P P J B O P J G D R L S H D E N D M
B N B P M P Q D R X H Y W T W D D G G M X
N S S E C C E N L T V P B B K X R A R W Y
J P F A H P O R M X E J Z D D K T C A Q R
V I K S M Y W N T V B N R J B L R I F M Q
H R D E G Z G Q S A S F T M Q T E E T V J
C A R D F F Y H E O I X B O H M U S E R V
B T T S R J A M L J R N A P U Z R W D C Q
N O M B S T B I T D M T S C B S T X L O X
C R H D E R E D N E G N E E G A S I V F N
A P R T M H C G A F N L W D P R N R N F X
Y U T N B N I E M P S N Y C E E O B O E J
W K G E N S G T X U T G Q R O N C M I R Q
C L W M N Y M K N I K H U D E V Q E T S K
S O Q E E A W K M S G G E M E E Q T A R L
T P G S L N W X D S U E H R U N Q T R F G
R S L I A R T N E A Z N N E L O W L O Y M
I L C T T P W E G N N T L T A M S E G U R
F E V S Y A P H D T G R L U T E V Z C G S
E Y N A K M T M L V F E N O I D N V L F B
K C R H B Z L I C D Y A Q C O Z Y K Z H V
B N J C H K Y Q O Y J T C C N V L V T N J
L G X W Y B W G M N V R Z A K S Z F Q Z B
P W D T J M N Z W L S E I G I D O R P S N
```

ACCOUTERED	COGITATIONS	ENTREAT	ORATION
AFFABILITY	CONSORTED	ENVENOMED	PORTENTOUS
APPEASED	CONSPIRATOR	EXIGENT	PRODIGIES
APPERTAIN	CONSTRUE	FAIN	PUISSANT
AUGMENTED	COVETOUS	INGRAFTED	STRIFE
AUGURERS	EMULATION	LEGACIES	VISAGE
BASE	ENGENDERED	MALICE	
CHASTISEMENT	ENSIGN	MANTLE	
COFFERS	ENTRAILS	METTLE	

Julius Caesar Vocabulary Word Search 4 Answer Key

Words are placed backwards, forward, diagonally, up and down. Words listed below are included in the maze. Circle the hidden vocabulary words in the maze.

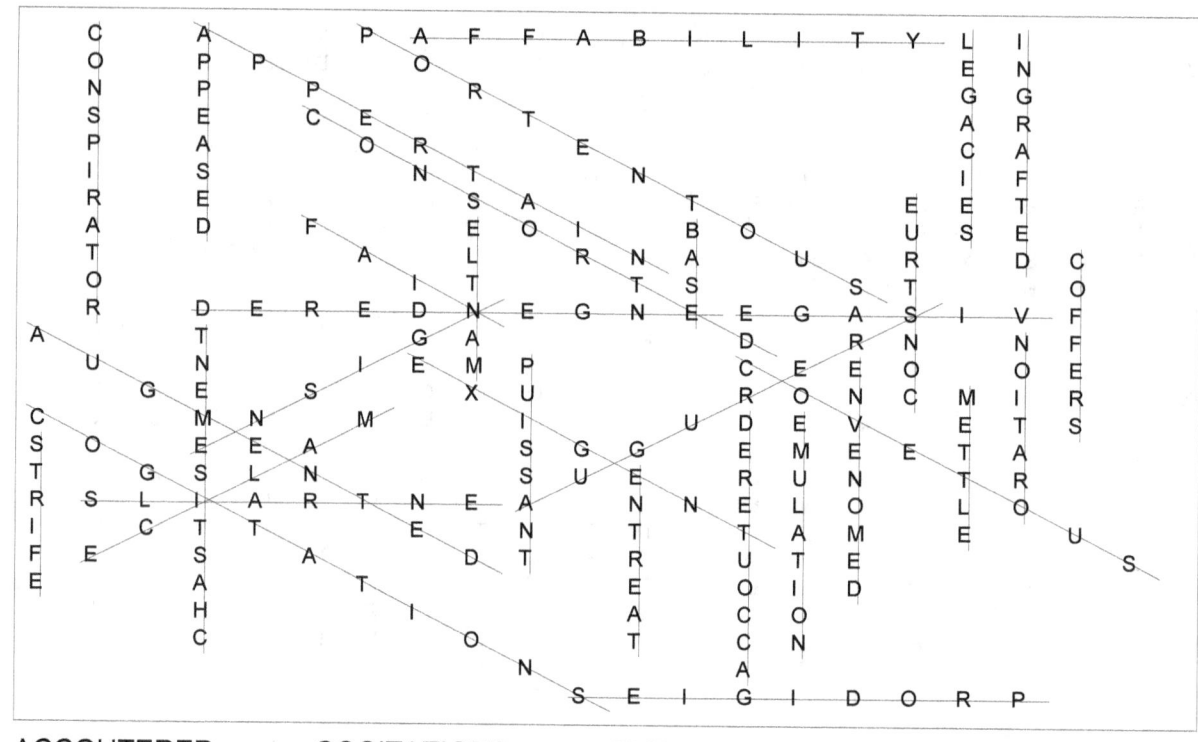

ACCOUTERED	COGITATIONS	ENTREAT	ORATION
AFFABILITY	CONSORTED	ENVENOMED	PORTENTOUS
APPEASED	CONSPIRATOR	EXIGENT	PRODIGIES
APPERTAIN	CONSTRUE	FAIN	PUISSANT
AUGMENTED	COVETOUS	INGRAFTED	STRIFE
AUGURERS	EMULATION	LEGACIES	VISAGE
BASE	ENGENDERED	MALICE	
CHASTISEMENT	ENSIGN	MANTLE	
COFFERS	ENTRAILS	METTLE	

Julius Caesar Vocabulary Crossword 1

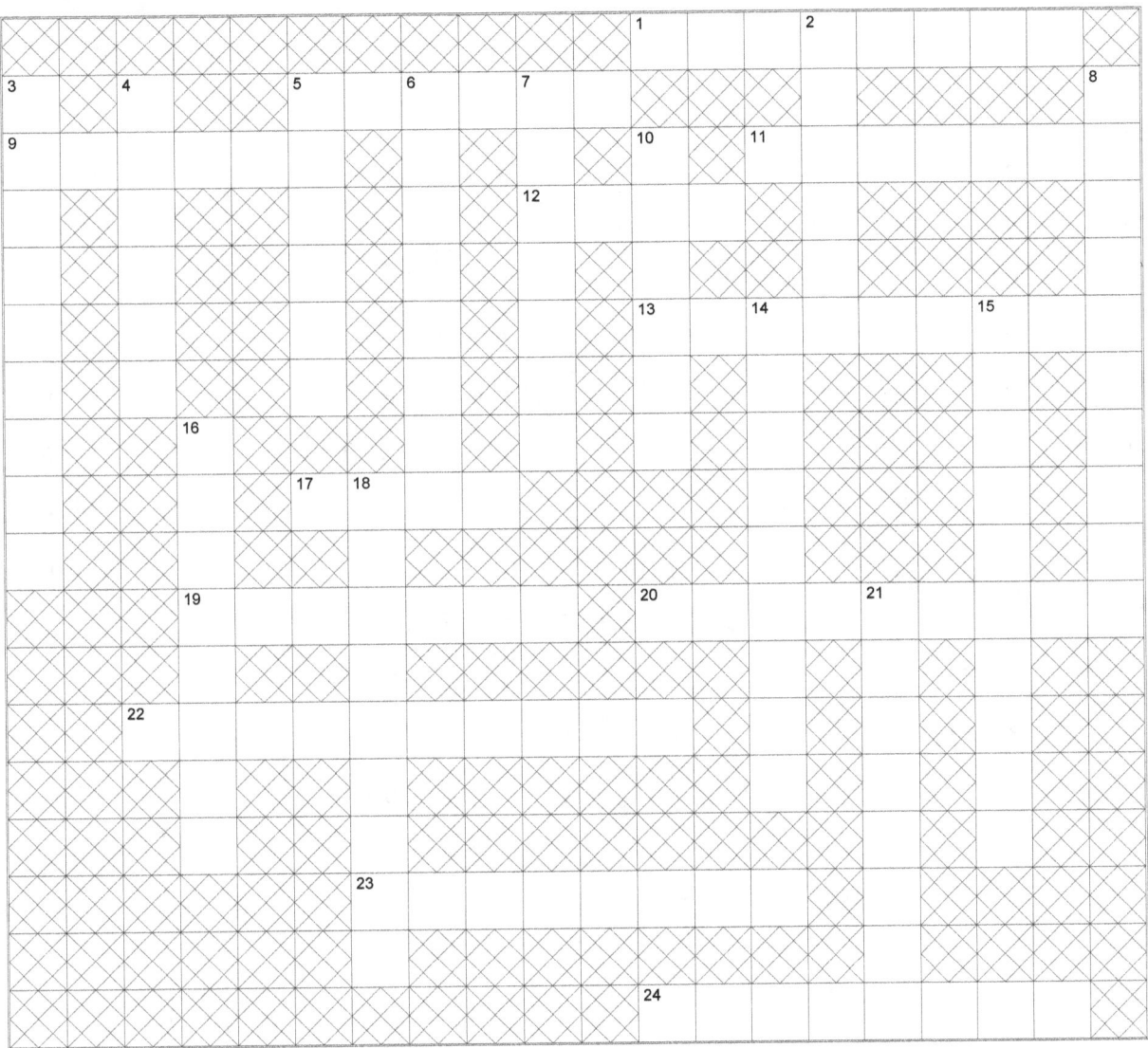

Across
1. Interpret
5. Ill-will or spite
9. Cloak; coat
11. Formal speech
12. Gladly
13. Belong to as a proper function or part
17. Without high values or ethics
19. Critical moment
20. Planted firmly; established
22. Foreboding
23. Internal organs, especially intestines
24. Powerful; mighty

Down
2. Struggle, fight, or quarrel
3. Envy; imitation
4. Colors; flag carried
5. Temperament
6. Inherited money or goods
7. Public treasury
8. Conceived
10. Face
14. Signs of disaster
15. Fully armed
16. Wanting the possessions of others
18. Made greater in size, extent, or quantity
21. Professional interpreters of omens

Julius Caesar Vocabulary Crossword 1 Answer Key

Across
1. Interpret
5. Ill-will or spite
9. Cloak; coat
11. Formal speech
12. Gladly
13. Belong to as a proper function or part
17. Without high values or ethics
19. Critical moment
20. Planted firmly; established
22. Foreboding
23. Internal organs, especially intestines
24. Powerful; mighty

Down
2. Struggle, fight, or quarrel
3. Envy; imitation
4. Colors; flag carried
5. Temperament
6. Inherited money or goods
7. Public treasury
8. Conceived
10. Face
14. Signs of disaster
15. Fully armed
16. Wanting the possessions of others
18. Made greater in size, extent, or quantity
21. Professional interpreters of omens

Julius Caesar Vocabulary Crossword 2

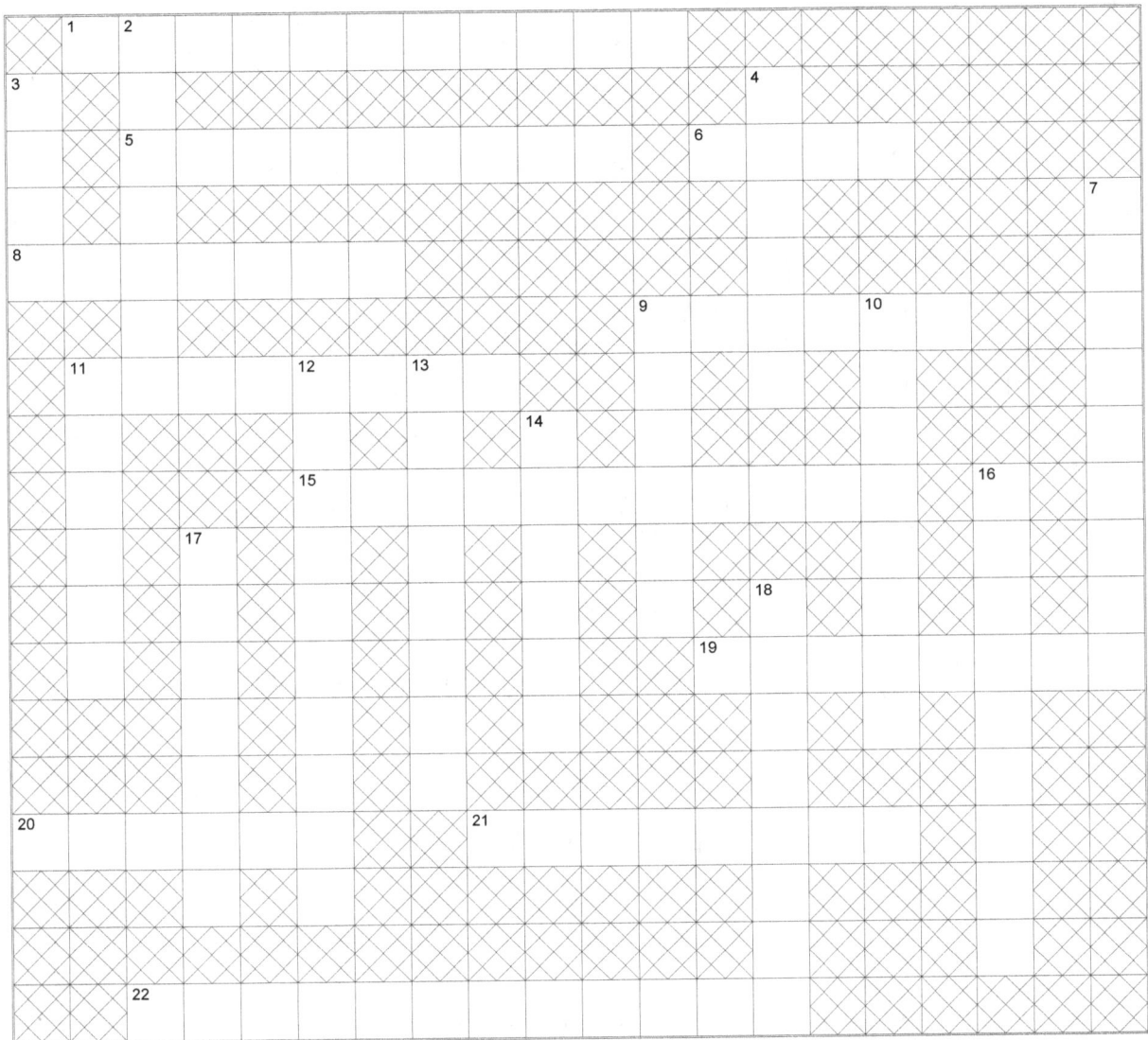

Across
1. One who plans with others to commit an illegal act
5. Made greater in size, extent, or quantity
6. Gladly
8. Critical moment
9. Ill-will or spite
11. Internal organs, especially intestines
15. Thoughts
19. Professional interpreters of omens
20. Face
21. Soothed; pacified
22. Punishment

Down
2. Formal speech
3. Without high values or ethics
4. Cloak; coat
7. Signs of disaster
9. Temperament
10. Interpret
11. Colors; flag carried
12. Fully armed
13. Inherited money or goods
14. Struggle, fight, or quarrel
16. Belong to as a proper function or part
17. Make an earnest request of
18. Powerful; mighty

Julius Caesar Vocabulary Crossword 2 Answer Key

Across
1. One who plans with others to commit an illegal act
5. Made greater in size, extent, or quantity
6. Gladly
8. Critical moment
9. Ill-will or spite
11. Internal organs, especially intestines
15. Thoughts
19. Professional interpreters of omens
20. Face
21. Soothed; pacified
22. Punishment

Down
2. Formal speech
3. Without high values or ethics
4. Cloak; coat
7. Signs of disaster
9. Temperament
10. Interpret
11. Colors; flag carried
12. Fully armed
13. Inherited money or goods
14. Struggle, fight, or quarrel
16. Belong to as a proper function or part
17. Make an earnest request of
18. Powerful; mighty

Answers

Across:
1. CONSPIRATOR
5. AUGMENTED
6. FAIN
8. EXIGENT
9. MALICE
11. ENTRAILS
15. COGITATIONS
19. AUGURERS
20. VISAGE
21. APPEASED
22. CHASTISEMENT

Down:
2. ORATION
3. BASE
4. MANTLE
7. PRODIGIES
9. METTLE
10. CONSTRUE
11. ENSIGNS
12. ATTRACTERED
13. LEGACIES
14. STRIFE
16. APPERTAIN
17. ENTREAT
18. PUISSANT

Julius Caesar Vocabulary Crossword 3

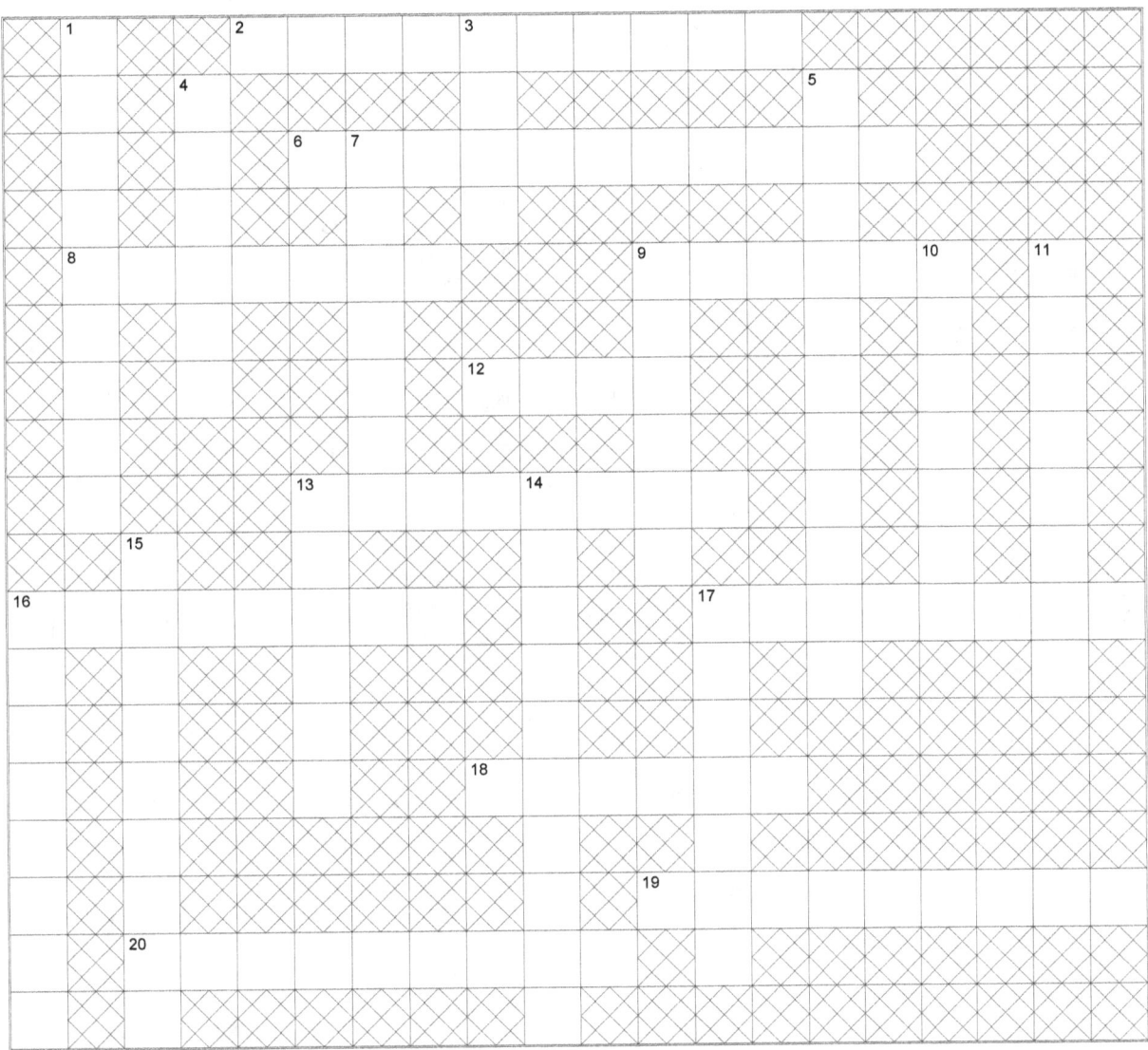

Across
2. Friendliness; graciousness
6. One who plans with others to commit an illegal act
8. Make an earnest request of
9. Ill-will or spite
12. Gladly
13. Internal organs, especially intestines
16. Soothed; pacified
17. Interpret
18. Struggle, fight, or quarrel
19. Signs of disaster
20. Planted firmly; established

Down
1. Made greater in size, extent, or quantity
3. Without high values or ethics
4. Temperament
5. Thoughts
7. Formal speech
9. Cloak; coat
10. Critical moment
11. Wanting the possessions of others
13. Colors; flag carried
14. Fully armed
15. Belong to as a proper function or part
16. Professional interpreters of omens
17. Public treasury

Julius Caesar Vocabulary Crossword 3 Answer Key

Across
2. Friendliness; graciousness
6. One who plans with others to commit an illegal act
8. Make an earnest request of
9. Ill-will or spite
12. Gladly
13. Internal organs, especially intestines
16. Soothed; pacified
17. Interpret
18. Struggle, fight, or quarrel
19. Signs of disaster
20. Planted firmly; established

Down
1. Made greater in size, extent, or quantity
3. Without high values or ethics
4. Temperament
5. Thoughts
7. Formal speech
9. Cloak; coat
10. Critical moment
11. Wanting the possessions of others
13. Colors; flag carried
14. Fully armed
15. Belong to as a proper function or part
16. Professional interpreters of omens
17. Public treasury

Julius Caesar Vocabulary Crossword 4

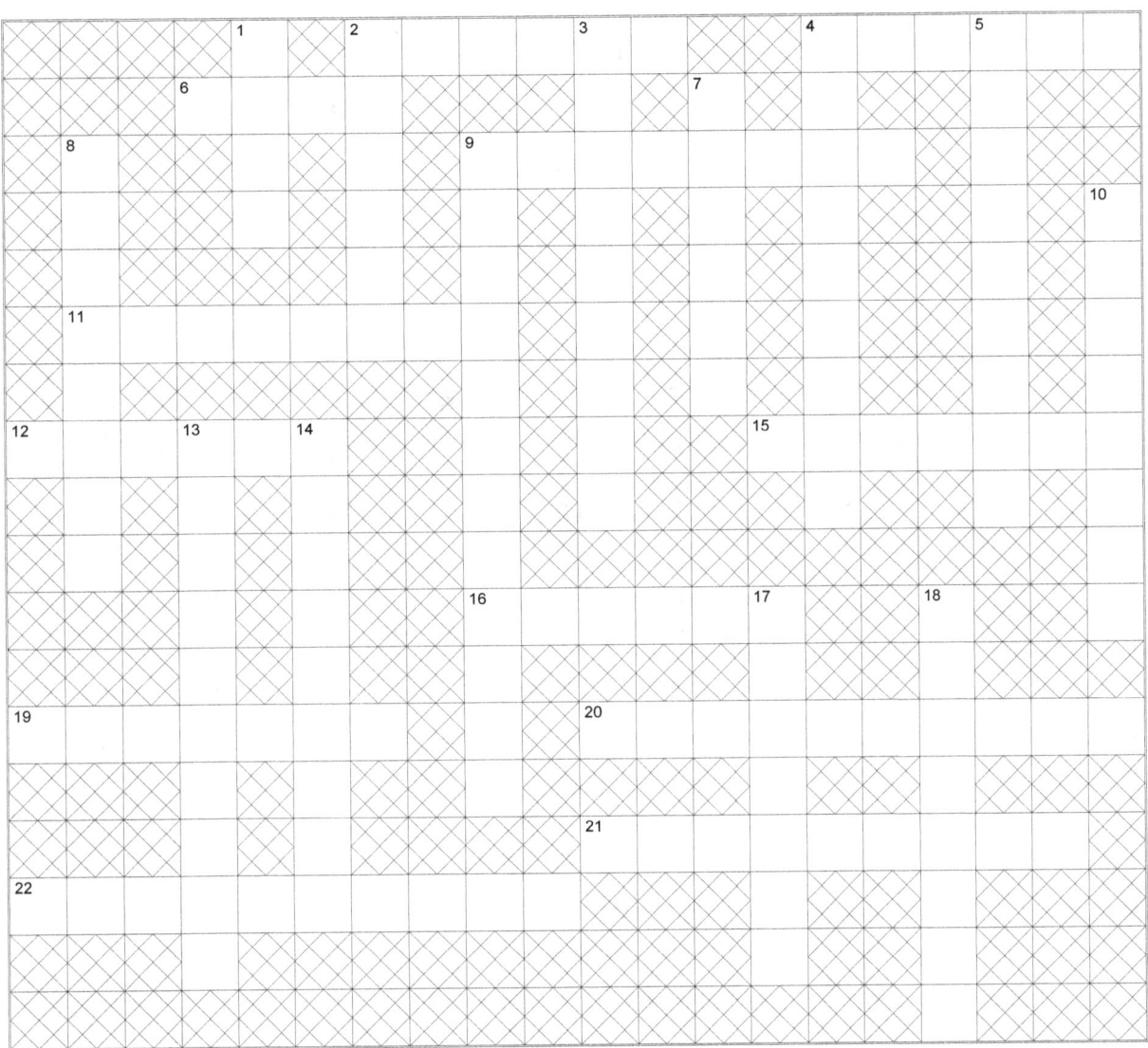

Across
2. Ill-will or spite
4. Colors; flag carried
6. Without high values or ethics
9. Interpret
11. Professional interpreters of omens
12. Face
15. Public treasury
16. Cloak; coat
19. Formal speech
20. Foreboding
21. Belong to as a proper function or part
22. Conceived

Down
1. Gladly
2. Temperament
3. Accompanied
4. Envy; imitation
5. Planted firmly; established
7. Struggle, fight, or quarrel
8. Inherited money or goods
9. Punishment
10. Powerful; mighty
13. Fully armed
14. Poisoned
17. Make an earnest request of
18. Internal organs, especially intestines

Julius Caesar Vocabulary Crossword 4 Answer Key

			1 F		2 M	A	L	I	3 C	E		4 E	N	S	5 I	G	N
		6 B	A	S	E				O		7 S	M			N		
	8 L		I		T		9 C	O	N	S	T	R	U	E	G		
	E		N		T		H		S		R		L		R		10 P
	G				L		A		O		I		A		A		U
	11 A	U	G	U	R	E	R	S			F		T		F		I
	C						T		T		E		I		T		S
12 V	I	S	13 A	G	14 E		I		E			15 C	O	F	F	E	R S
	E		C		N		S		D			O			D		A
	S		C		V		E					N					N
			O		E		16 M	A	N	T	L	17 E		18 E			T
			U		N		E					N		N			
19 O	R	A	T	I	O	N		20 P	O	R	T	E	N	T	O	U	S
			E		M			T				R		R			
			R		E		21 A	P	P	E	R	T	A	I	N		
22 E	N	G	E	N	D	E	R	E	D			A		I			
			D									T		L			
														S			

Across
2. Ill-will or spite
4. Colors; flag carried
6. Without high values or ethics
9. Interpret
11. Professional interpreters of omens
12. Face
15. Public treasury
16. Cloak; coat
19. Formal speech
20. Foreboding
21. Belong to as a proper function or part
22. Conceived

Down
1. Gladly
2. Temperament
3. Accompanied
4. Envy; imitation
5. Planted firmly; established
7. Struggle, fight, or quarrel
8. Inherited money or goods
9. Punishment
10. Powerful; mighty
13. Fully armed
14. Poisoned
17. Make an earnest request of
18. Internal organs, especially intestines

Julius Caesar Vocabulary Juggle Letters 1

1. OSNTRCODE = 1. _____
   Accompanied

2. GUEARURS = 2. _____
   Professional interpreters of omens

3. VUCETOSO = 3. _____
   Wanting the possessions of others

4. REITFS = 4. _____
   Struggle, fight, or quarrel

5. NGEFDTIRA = 5. _____
   Planted firmly; established

6. TELTME = 6. _____
   Temperament

7. ISNEETSHAMCT = 7. _____
   Punishment

8. ANFI = 8. _____
   Gladly

9. SNTUSIPA = 9. _____
   Powerful; mighty

10. EAGISCLE = 10. _____
    Inherited money or goods

11. BSAE = 11. _____
    Without high values or ethics

12. FCROFSE = 12. _____
    Public treasury

13. AEILUTMNO = 13. _____
    Envy

14. UNTMGEDEA = 14. _____
    Made greater in size, extent, or quantity

15. RCEADUOCTE = 15. _____
    Fully armed

Julius Caesar Vocabulary Juggle Letters 1 Answer Key

1. OSNTRCODE = 1. CONSORTED
   Accompanied

2. GUEARURS = 2. AUGURERS
   Professional interpreters of omens

3. VUCETOSO = 3. COVETOUS
   Wanting the possessions of others

4. REITFS = 4. STRIFE
   Struggle, fight, or quarrel

5. NGEFDTIRA = 5. INGRAFTED
   Planted firmly; established

6. TELTME = 6. METTLE
   Temperament

7. ISNEETSHAMCT = 7. CHASTISEMENT
   Punishment

8. ANFI = 8. FAIN
   Gladly

9. SNTUSIPA = 9. PUISSANT
   Powerful; mighty

10. EAGISCLE = 10. LEGACIES
    Inherited money or goods

11. BSAE = 11. BASE
    Without high values or ethics

12. FCROFSE = 12. COFFERS
    Public treasury

13. AEILUTMNO = 13. EMULATION
    Envy; imitating

14. UNTMGEDEA = 14. AUGMENTED
    Made greater in size, extent, or quantity

15. RCEADUOCTE = 15. ACCOUTERED
    Fully armed

Julius Caesar Vocabulary Juggle Letters 2

1. BFIATALYFI = 1. _____
   Friendliness; graciousness

2. GDNEEEDNER = 2. _____
   Conceived

3. REEACDCUTO = 3. _____
   Fully armed

4. SEANRTIL = 4. _____
   Internal organs, especially intestines

5. ECFOSRF = 5. _____
   Public treasury

6. ESFTIR = 6. _____
   Struggle, fight, or quarrel

7. REDGIATNF = 7. _____
   Planted firmly; established

8. VODENEENM = 8. _____
   Poisoned

9. STUROECN = 9. _____
   Interpret

10. ETSONORDC = 10. _____
    Accompanied

11. SNEING = 11. _____
    Colors; flag carried

12. GLESECIA = 12. _____
    Inherited money or goods

13. SAPTCIROONR = 13. _____
    One who plans with others to commit an illegal act

14. IFAN = 14. _____
    Gladly

15. GUAESRUR = 15. _____
    Professional interpreters of omens

Julius Caesar Vocabulary Juggle Letters 2 Answer Key

1. BFIATALYFI = 1. AFFABILITY
   Friendliness; graciousness

2. GDNEEEDNER = 2. ENGENDERED
   Conceived

3. REEACDCUTO = 3. ACCOUTERED
   Fully armed

4. SEANRTIL = 4. ENTRAILS
   Internal organs, especially intestines

5. ECFOSRF = 5. COFFERS
   Public treasury

6. ESFTIR = 6. STRIFE
   Struggle, fight, or quarrel

7. REDGIATNF = 7. INGRAFTED
   Planted firmly; established

8. VODENEENM = 8. ENVENOMED
   Poisoned

9. STUROECN = 9. CONSTRUE
   Interpret

10. ETSONORDC = 10. CONSORTED
    Accompanied

11. SNEING = 11. ENSIGN
    Colors; flag carried

12. GLESECIA = 12. LEGACIES
    Inherited money or goods

13. SAPTCIROONR = 13. CONSPIRATOR
    One who plans with others to commit an illegal act

14. IFAN = 14. FAIN
    Gladly

15. GUAESRUR = 15. AUGURERS
    Professional interpreters of omens

Julius Caesar Vocabulary Juggle Letters 3

1. NRTEAET = 1. _____
   Make an earnest request of

2. UCNOERST = 2. _____
   Interpret

3. LTNEAM = 3. _____
   Cloak; coat

4. AMOITELUN = 4. _____
   Envy

5. INTTAHCSESEM = 5. _____
   Punishment

6. LATERNSI = 6. _____
   Internal organs, especially intestines

7. ESGIVA = 7. _____
   Face

8. NNIESG = 8. _____
   Colors; flag carried

9. OTPORARNCIS = 9. _____
   One who plans with others to commit an illegal act

10. RIONOTA = 10. _____
    Formal speech

11. AFNI = 11. _____
    Gladly

12. DTOEARECCU = 12. _____
    Fully armed

13. SSNPUAIT = 13. _____
    Powerful; mighty

14. ESBA = 14. _____
    Without high values or ethics

15. FSCRFOE = 15. _____
    Public treasury

Julius Caesar Vocabulary Juggle Letters 3 Answer Key

1. NRTEAET = 1. ENTREAT
   Make an earnest request of

2. UCNOERST = 2. CONSTRUE
   Interpret

3. LTNEAM = 3. MANTLE
   Cloak; coat

4. AMOITELUN = 4. EMULATION
   Envy

5. INTTAHCSESEM = 5. CHASTISEMENT
   Punishment

6. LATERNSI = 6. ENTRAILS
   Internal organs, especially intestines

7. ESGIVA = 7. VISAGE
   Face

8. NNIESG = 8. ENSIGN
   Colors; flag carried

9. OTPORARNCIS = 9. CONSPIRATOR
   One who plans with others to commit an illegal act

10. RIONOTA = 10. ORATION
    Formal speech

11. AFNI = 11. FAIN
    Gladly

12. DTOEARECCU = 12. ACCOUTERED
    Fully armed

13. SSNPUAIT = 13. PUISSANT
    Powerful; mighty

14. ESBA = 14. BASE
    Without high values or ethics

15. FSCRFOE = 15. COFFERS
    Public treasury

Julius Caesar Vocabulary Juggle Letters 4

1. OIROANT = 1. _____
   Formal speech

2. ENDROSCTO = 2. _____
   Accompanied

3. ENVDOEMEN = 3. _____
   Poisoned

4. IYTLIFAABF = 4. _____
   Friendliness; graciousness

5. OMTNALEUI = 5. _____
   Envy

6. UACETRODCE = 6. _____
   Fully armed

7. AEGISV = 7. _____
   Face

8. ENSAHMTESTCI = 8. _____
   Punishment

9. UGURAESR = 9. _____
   Professional interpreters of omens

10. REOPONTTSU = 10. _____
    Foreboding

11. TENLAM = 11. _____
    Cloak; coat

12. ASIGTNCOITO = 12. _____
    Thoughts

13. ACEMLI = 13. _____
    Ill-will or spite

14. IANF = 14. _____
    Gladly

15. DMNUAETEG = 15. _____
    Made greater in size, extent, or quantity

Julius Caesar Vocabulary Juggle Letters 4 Answer Key

1. OIROANT = 1. ORATION
Formal speech

2. ENDROSCTO = 2. CONSORTED
Accompanied

3. ENVDOEMEN = 3. ENVENOMED
Poisoned

4. IYTLIFAABF = 4. AFFABILITY
Friendliness; graciousness

5. OMTNALEUI = 5. EMULATION
Envy

6. UACETRODCE = 6. ACCOUTERED
Fully armed

7. AEGISV = 7. VISAGE
Face

8. ENSAHMTESTCI = 8. CHASTISEMENT
Punishment

9. UGURAESR = 9. AUGURERS
Professional interpreters of omens

10. REOPONTTSU =10. PORTENTOUS
Foreboding

11. TENLAM =11. MANTLE
Cloak; coat

12. ASIGTNCOITO =12. COGITATIONS
Thoughts

13. ACEMLI =13. MALICE
Ill-will or spite

14. IANF =14. FAIN
Gladly

15. DMNUAETEG =15. AUGMENTED
Made greater in size, extent, or quantity

ACCOUTERED	Fully armed
AFFABILITY	Friendliness; graciousness
APPEASED	Soothed; pacified
APPERTAIN	Belong to as a proper function or part
AUGMENTED	Made greater in size, extent, or quantity
AUGURERS	Professional interpreters of omens

BASE	Without high values or ethics
CHASTISEMENT	Punishment
COFFERS	Public treasury
COGITATIONS	Thoughts
CONSORTED	Accompanied
CONSPIRATOR	One who plans with others to commit an illegal act

CONSTRUE	Interpret
COVETOUS	Wanting the possessions of others
EMULATION	Envy; imitating
ENGENDERED	Conceived
ENSIGN	Colors; flag carried
ENTRAILS	Internal organs, especially intestines

ENTREAT	Make an earnest request of
ENVENOMED	Poisoned
EXIGENT	Critical moment
FAIN	Gladly
INGRAFTED	Planted firmly; established
LEGACIES	Inherited money or goods

MALICE	Ill-will or spite
MANTLE	Cloak; coat
METTLE	Temperament
ORATION	Formal speech
PORTENTOUS	Foreboding
PRODIGIES	Signs of disaster

PUISSANT	Powerful; mighty
STRIFE	Struggle, fight, or quarrel
VISAGE	Face

Julius Caesar Vocabulary

MANTLE	EXIGENT	MALICE	ENSIGN	ENGENDERED
EMULATION	PRODIGIES	PUISSANT	APPERTAIN	AFFABILITY
VISAGE	COFFERS	FREE SPACE	AUGMENTED	CONSPIRATOR
APPEASED	COGITATIONS	LEGACIES	METTLE	FAIN
BASE	PORTENTOUS	ENVENOMED	CONSTRUE	AUGURERS

Julius Caesar Vocabulary

ENTREAT	CHASTISEMENT	CONSORTED	COVETOUS	INGRAFTED
ACCOUTERED	ORATION	ENTRAILS	AUGURERS	CONSTRUE
ENVENOMED	PORTENTOUS	FREE SPACE	FAIN	METTLE
LEGACIES	COGITATIONS	APPEASED	CONSPIRATOR	AUGMENTED
STRIFE	COFFERS	VISAGE	AFFABILITY	APPERTAIN

Julius Caesar Vocabulary

COGITATIONS	STRIFE	METTLE	VISAGE	LEGACIES
ORATION	ENVENOMED	COFFERS	INGRAFTED	CONSPIRATOR
APPERTAIN	CHASTISEMENT	FREE SPACE	MANTLE	COVETOUS
MALICE	PUISSANT	CONSORTED	EXIGENT	ENTREAT
PRODIGIES	ENSIGN	PORTENTOUS	ACCOUTERED	AFFABILITY

Julius Caesar Vocabulary

APPEASED	AUGURERS	BASE	AUGMENTED	EMULATION
ENGENDERED	FAIN	CONSTRUE	AFFABILITY	ACCOUTERED
PORTENTOUS	ENSIGN	FREE SPACE	ENTREAT	EXIGENT
CONSORTED	PUISSANT	MALICE	COVETOUS	MANTLE
ENTRAILS	CHASTISEMENT	APPERTAIN	CONSPIRATOR	INGRAFTED

Julius Caesar Vocabulary

VISAGE	AFFABILITY	ENVENOMED	ENGENDERED	MANTLE
LEGACIES	BASE	CONSPIRATOR	EXIGENT	ORATION
APPERTAIN	COGITATIONS	FREE SPACE	STRIFE	INGRAFTED
COFFERS	EMULATION	ENTREAT	FAIN	ACCOUTERED
PUISSANT	ENTRAILS	APPEASED	CHASTISEMENT	AUGMENTED

Julius Caesar Vocabulary

ENSIGN	CONSTRUE	PORTENTOUS	AUGURERS	CONSORTED
MALICE	METTLE	PRODIGIES	AUGMENTED	CHASTISEMENT
APPEASED	ENTRAILS	FREE SPACE	ACCOUTERED	FAIN
ENTREAT	EMULATION	COFFERS	INGRAFTED	STRIFE
COVETOUS	COGITATIONS	APPERTAIN	ORATION	EXIGENT

Julius Caesar Vocabulary

AUGMENTED	EMULATION	ACCOUTERED	CONSTRUE	APPEASED
EXIGENT	ENTRAILS	MALICE	METTLE	CONSORTED
STRIFE	AFFABILITY	FREE SPACE	FAIN	MANTLE
ORATION	COFFERS	APPERTAIN	PORTENTOUS	COGITATIONS
ENTREAT	ENGENDERED	ENVENOMED	LEGACIES	INGRAFTED

Julius Caesar Vocabulary

PRODIGIES	PUISSANT	ENSIGN	BASE	COVETOUS
CONSPIRATOR	CHASTISEMENT	VISAGE	INGRAFTED	LEGACIES
ENVENOMED	ENGENDERED	FREE SPACE	COGITATIONS	PORTENTOUS
APPERTAIN	COFFERS	ORATION	MANTLE	FAIN
AUGURERS	AFFABILITY	STRIFE	CONSORTED	METTLE

Julius Caesar Vocabulary

COVETOUS	APPERTAIN	ORATION	CONSPIRATOR	VISAGE
STRIFE	PUISSANT	AFFABILITY	ENTRAILS	ENTREAT
MANTLE	ACCOUTERED	FREE SPACE	PORTENTOUS	LEGACIES
MALICE	ENSIGN	EMULATION	PRODIGIES	ENGENDERED
CHASTISEMENT	AUGMENTED	ENVENOMED	FAIN	METTLE

Julius Caesar Vocabulary

INGRAFTED	AUGURERS	COGITATIONS	COFFERS	EXIGENT
CONSTRUE	APPEASED	BASE	METTLE	FAIN
ENVENOMED	AUGMENTED	FREE SPACE	ENGENDERED	PRODIGIES
EMULATION	ENSIGN	MALICE	LEGACIES	PORTENTOUS
CONSORTED	ACCOUTERED	MANTLE	ENTREAT	ENTRAILS

Julius Caesar Vocabulary

INGRAFTED	MALICE	APPEASED	FAIN	CONSTRUE
COGITATIONS	STRIFE	CHASTISEMENT	AUGMENTED	ENSIGN
PUISSANT	AUGURERS	FREE SPACE	MANTLE	BASE
ENGENDERED	VISAGE	EXIGENT	EMULATION	PRODIGIES
CONSPIRATOR	COVETOUS	METTLE	AFFABILITY	COFFERS

Julius Caesar Vocabulary

ORATION	ENTRAILS	ENTREAT	APPERTAIN	PORTENTOUS
ACCOUTERED	LEGACIES	CONSORTED	COFFERS	AFFABILITY
METTLE	COVETOUS	FREE SPACE	PRODIGIES	EMULATION
EXIGENT	VISAGE	ENGENDERED	BASE	MANTLE
ENVENOMED	AUGURERS	PUISSANT	ENSIGN	AUGMENTED

Julius Caesar Vocabulary

ENGENDERED	ACCOUTERED	PUISSANT	EMULATION	INGRAFTED
MALICE	PORTENTOUS	LEGACIES	AUGURERS	BASE
ORATION	APPEASED	FREE SPACE	ENTREAT	ENTRAILS
CONSTRUE	VISAGE	ENVENOMED	METTLE	COGITATIONS
AFFABILITY	FAIN	MANTLE	COFFERS	AUGMENTED

Julius Caesar Vocabulary

CHASTISEMENT	CONSPIRATOR	EXIGENT	APPERTAIN	PRODIGIES
ENSIGN	CONSORTED	STRIFE	AUGMENTED	COFFERS
MANTLE	FAIN	FREE SPACE	COGITATIONS	METTLE
ENVENOMED	VISAGE	CONSTRUE	ENTRAILS	ENTREAT
COVETOUS	APPEASED	ORATION	BASE	AUGURERS

Julius Caesar Vocabulary

ENVENOMED	CHASTISEMENT	ACCOUTERED	PRODIGIES	AUGMENTED
CONSORTED	COVETOUS	EXIGENT	AUGURERS	COFFERS
CONSPIRATOR	ENTREAT	FREE SPACE	ENTRAILS	APPERTAIN
EMULATION	METTLE	PUISSANT	PORTENTOUS	INGRAFTED
COGITATIONS	CONSTRUE	ENGENDERED	BASE	LEGACIES

Julius Caesar Vocabulary

MALICE	VISAGE	FAIN	STRIFE	ENSIGN
MANTLE	AFFABILITY	ORATION	LEGACIES	BASE
ENGENDERED	CONSTRUE	FREE SPACE	INGRAFTED	PORTENTOUS
PUISSANT	METTLE	EMULATION	APPERTAIN	ENTRAILS
APPEASED	ENTREAT	CONSPIRATOR	COFFERS	AUGURERS

Julius Caesar Vocabulary

CONSPIRATOR	INGRAFTED	AFFABILITY	APPEASED	ENTRAILS
FAIN	APPERTAIN	EMULATION	VISAGE	EXIGENT
ACCOUTERED	AUGURERS	FREE SPACE	COFFERS	PORTENTOUS
MANTLE	COGITATIONS	ENVENOMED	ENTREAT	AUGMENTED
CHASTISEMENT	ENSIGN	ENGENDERED	ORATION	LEGACIES

Julius Caesar Vocabulary

CONSORTED	CONSTRUE	BASE	METTLE	PUISSANT
STRIFE	COVETOUS	MALICE	LEGACIES	ORATION
ENGENDERED	ENSIGN	FREE SPACE	AUGMENTED	ENTREAT
ENVENOMED	COGITATIONS	MANTLE	PORTENTOUS	COFFERS
PRODIGIES	AUGURERS	ACCOUTERED	EXIGENT	VISAGE

Julius Caesar Vocabulary

EMULATION	ENVENOMED	COGITATIONS	ENTRAILS	STRIFE
ENTREAT	LEGACIES	CHASTISEMENT	COVETOUS	VISAGE
ORATION	CONSPIRATOR	FREE SPACE	METTLE	PUISSANT
INGRAFTED	ACCOUTERED	CONSORTED	MALICE	EXIGENT
ENSIGN	COFFERS	APPERTAIN	PORTENTOUS	ENGENDERED

Julius Caesar Vocabulary

PRODIGIES	APPEASED	MANTLE	AUGURERS	BASE
AUGMENTED	FAIN	CONSTRUE	ENGENDERED	PORTENTOUS
APPERTAIN	COFFERS	FREE SPACE	EXIGENT	MALICE
CONSORTED	ACCOUTERED	INGRAFTED	PUISSANT	METTLE
AFFABILITY	CONSPIRATOR	ORATION	VISAGE	COVETOUS

Julius Caesar Vocabulary

CONSORTED	COFFERS	MANTLE	COGITATIONS	CONSPIRATOR
BASE	STRIFE	PORTENTOUS	CONSTRUE	COVETOUS
INGRAFTED	ENTRAILS	FREE SPACE	AUGMENTED	FAIN
EXIGENT	ENGENDERED	ACCOUTERED	APPEASED	ENVENOMED
ORATION	ENSIGN	MALICE	ENTREAT	CHASTISEMENT

Julius Caesar Vocabulary

LEGACIES	METTLE	AUGURERS	PRODIGIES	PUISSANT
EMULATION	VISAGE	APPERTAIN	CHASTISEMENT	ENTREAT
MALICE	ENSIGN	FREE SPACE	ENVENOMED	APPEASED
ACCOUTERED	ENGENDERED	EXIGENT	FAIN	AUGMENTED
AFFABILITY	ENTRAILS	INGRAFTED	COVETOUS	CONSTRUE

Julius Caesar Vocabulary

ORATION	LEGACIES	AUGMENTED	CHASTISEMENT	VISAGE
MANTLE	ACCOUTERED	PUISSANT	APPERTAIN	INGRAFTED
ENTRAILS	METTLE	FREE SPACE	COGITATIONS	PRODIGIES
MALICE	ENGENDERED	BASE	EXIGENT	STRIFE
COFFERS	ENTREAT	FAIN	CONSORTED	PORTENTOUS

Julius Caesar Vocabulary

APPEASED	AFFABILITY	CONSPIRATOR	COVETOUS	AUGURERS
EMULATION	CONSTRUE	ENVENOMED	PORTENTOUS	CONSORTED
FAIN	ENTREAT	FREE SPACE	STRIFE	EXIGENT
BASE	ENGENDERED	MALICE	PRODIGIES	COGITATIONS
ENSIGN	METTLE	ENTRAILS	INGRAFTED	APPERTAIN

Julius Caesar Vocabulary

EXIGENT	ENVENOMED	FAIN	APPERTAIN	CONSTRUE
ENGENDERED	EMULATION	MALICE	MANTLE	INGRAFTED
STRIFE	CONSORTED	FREE SPACE	CONSPIRATOR	APPEASED
ACCOUTERED	ENTREAT	LEGACIES	COGITATIONS	METTLE
PRODIGIES	AUGMENTED	CHASTISEMENT	AFFABILITY	ENSIGN

Julius Caesar Vocabulary

ENTRAILS	PUISSANT	BASE	AUGURERS	PORTENTOUS
VISAGE	COVETOUS	COFFERS	ENSIGN	AFFABILITY
CHASTISEMENT	AUGMENTED	FREE SPACE	METTLE	COGITATIONS
LEGACIES	ENTREAT	ACCOUTERED	APPEASED	CONSPIRATOR
ORATION	CONSORTED	STRIFE	INGRAFTED	MANTLE

Julius Caesar Vocabulary

COVETOUS	ENSIGN	CONSTRUE	BASE	EXIGENT
CHASTISEMENT	MANTLE	LEGACIES	EMULATION	APPERTAIN
COFFERS	PORTENTOUS	FREE SPACE	FAIN	CONSORTED
COGITATIONS	AFFABILITY	ENTREAT	METTLE	CONSPIRATOR
AUGURERS	AUGMENTED	ENTRAILS	STRIFE	PUISSANT

Julius Caesar Vocabulary

VISAGE	INGRAFTED	APPEASED	ACCOUTERED	MALICE
ENGENDERED	PRODIGIES	ORATION	PUISSANT	STRIFE
ENTRAILS	AUGMENTED	FREE SPACE	CONSPIRATOR	METTLE
ENTREAT	AFFABILITY	COGITATIONS	CONSORTED	FAIN
ENVENOMED	PORTENTOUS	COFFERS	APPERTAIN	EMULATION

Julius Caesar Vocabulary

VISAGE	CONSORTED	INGRAFTED	ENTREAT	ENTRAILS
COGITATIONS	LEGACIES	AUGMENTED	APPEASED	CHASTISEMENT
COVETOUS	BASE	FREE SPACE	FAIN	APPERTAIN
CONSTRUE	PUISSANT	AFFABILITY	AUGURERS	EMULATION
EXIGENT	MALICE	ACCOUTERED	MANTLE	ORATION

Julius Caesar Vocabulary

CONSPIRATOR	ENGENDERED	ENVENOMED	PRODIGIES	ENSIGN
COFFERS	STRIFE	PORTENTOUS	ORATION	MANTLE
ACCOUTERED	MALICE	FREE SPACE	EMULATION	AUGURERS
AFFABILITY	PUISSANT	CONSTRUE	APPERTAIN	FAIN
METTLE	BASE	COVETOUS	CHASTISEMENT	APPEASED

Julius Caesar Vocabulary

EMULATION	ENTREAT	COVETOUS	METTLE	PRODIGIES
APPEASED	MANTLE	ACCOUTERED	ENVENOMED	FAIN
CONSPIRATOR	MALICE	FREE SPACE	STRIFE	CONSTRUE
AUGMENTED	ENGENDERED	APPERTAIN	ENSIGN	PUISSANT
CHASTISEMENT	INGRAFTED	EXIGENT	LEGACIES	BASE

Julius Caesar Vocabulary

PORTENTOUS	AFFABILITY	VISAGE	COGITATIONS	CONSORTED
COFFERS	ORATION	ENTRAILS	BASE	LEGACIES
EXIGENT	INGRAFTED	FREE SPACE	PUISSANT	ENSIGN
APPERTAIN	ENGENDERED	AUGMENTED	CONSTRUE	STRIFE
AUGURERS	MALICE	CONSPIRATOR	FAIN	ENVENOMED

www.ingramcontent.com/pod-product-compliance
Lightning Source LLC
Chambersburg PA
CBHW081457070526
44586CB00019B/2390